T0382815

ROUTLEDGE LIBRARY EDITIONS:
ACCOUNTING HISTORY

Volume 13

A COMMON-SENSE METHOD OF DOUBLE-ENTRY BOOKKEEPING ON FIRST PRINCIPLES

A COMMON-SENSE METHOD OF DOUBLE-ENTRY BOOKKEEPING ON FIRST PRINCIPLES

As Suggested by De Morgan. Part 1 Theoretical

S. DYER

Routledge
Taylor & Francis Group

LONDON AND NEW YORK

First published in 1984 by Garland Publishing, Inc.

This edition first published in 2021
by Routledge
2 Park Square, Milton Park, Abingdon, Oxon OX14 4RN

and by Routledge
52 Vanderbilt Avenue, New York, NY 10017

Routledge is an imprint of the Taylor & Francis Group, an informa business

British Library Cataloguing in Publication Data
A catalogue record for this book is available from the British Library

ISBN: 978-0-367-33564-9 (Set)
ISBN: 978-1-00-304636-3 (Set) (ebk)
ISBN: 978-0-367-50509-7 (Volume 13) (hbk)
ISBN: 978-1-00-305017-9 (Volume 13) (ebk)

Publisher's Note
The publisher has gone to great lengths to ensure the quality of this reprint but
points out that some imperfections in the original copies may be apparent.

Disclaimer
The publisher has made every effort to trace copyright holders and would welcome
correspondence from those they have been unable to trace.

A Common-Sense Method of Double-Entry Bookkeeping on First Principles

As Suggested by De Morgan

Part I
Theoretical

S. Dyer

GARLAND PUBLISHING, INC.
NEW YORK & LONDON 1984

For a complete list of the titles in this series
see the final pages of this volume.

This facsimile has been made from a copy in
the New York Public Library.

Library of Congress Cataloging in Publication Data

Dyer, S.
A common-sense method of double-entry bookkeeping on
first principles, as suggested by De Morgan.

(Accounting history and the development of a
profession)
Reprint of v. 1. Originally published: London :
G. Philip, 1897.
1. Bookkeeping—History.   2. Accounting—History.
3. De Morgan, Augustus, 1806–1871.   I. Title.
II. Series.
HF5611.D94   1984   657'.2   82-48384
ISBN 0-8240-6324-4 (alk. paper)

The volumes in this series are printed on
acid-free, 250-year-life paper.

Printed in the United States of America

A COMMON-SENSE METHOD

OF

DOUBLE-ENTRY BOOKKEEPING

ON FIRST PRINCIPLES.

As Suggested by DE MORGAN.

PART I.—THEORETICAL.

CONTAINING A SIMPLIFIED COMMON-SENSE PRESENTMENT OF
DR. AND CR., THE PERFECT FORM OF TRIAL BALANCE,
AND THE FOUR METHODS OF PROVING BOOKS.

BY

S. DYER

UNIV. LONDON.

LONDON

GEORGE PHILIP & SON, 32, FLEET STREET, E.C.

LIVERPOOL: PHILIP, SON, & NEPHEW, 45 TO 51, SOUTH CASTLE STREET

1897

INTRODUCTION.

THIS book makes no pretensions whatever, except as the exponent of a common-sense method of teaching Bookkeeping. *This* its Author owes to De Morgan, and he is prepared to stand by it, as by an old friend, against all comers. He submits it as a system easier to teach and pleasanter to learn than any other known to teachers. It is *Bookkeeping on First Principles*. Its constant precept is "Look to the end; make no entry without considering what effect that entry will have on the Final Balance Sheet, and *why* it must have that effect."

The author considers as of the essence of the method, (1) the separation into *two Sets* of the Ledger Accounts in the Trial Balance; (2) the unvarying sequence of these accounts; and (3) the completion of the Trial Balance by debiting the value of Goods left unsold to Valuation account and crediting it to Trade account before adding up. Whatever theorists may think of it, children readily understand it, and like it. The method presupposes the Ledger to be taught first, as being more pictorial than the Journal, and, as the French call it, *Le Grand Livre*. In class teaching, two large blackboards are necessary, one for the Double-Entry accounts, the other, placed on the opposite side of the class, for the Single-Entry accounts. Until pupils can work an easy Examination Paper in Bookkeeping, ordinary foolscap, or a close-lined exercise book, a little broader than long, is much better than specially prepared paper. Results, in every exercise, should be tested in at least two ways. In posting, the Journal can be taught orally long before written journalising is begun; and classified journalising is recommended. So also the constant practice of compiling the Final Balance Sheet and all the Final Results from the Trial Balance without closing books.

Class Teachers will find here short easy exercises to base their demonstrations upon; short enough to be posted, tested, balanced, and closed during a single lesson; and varied so as to embrace, step by step, every ordinary difficulty. Private students will find a common-sense explanation of every fresh entry, and clear directions given at the moment of need. In the Theoretical Part, special care has been bestowed on the Profit and Loss items, and the whole theory of Double-Entry.

Teachers wishing to communicate with the Author are invited to do so through the Publishers. Suggestions from teachers for the improvement of the book will be cordially welcomed, and acted upon when possible.

CONTENTS.

BOOKKEEPING DIAGRAMS

FOR CLASS TEACHING.

CONSPECTUS OF

THE DOUBLE-ENTRY ACCOUNTS.

i.e. My own (the Proprietor's) accounts.

Dr AGAINST ME.	IN MY FAVOUR. C^r

Capital Account.

Private Expenses (withdrawals).	Initial Net Capital.
Interest charged on ditto.	Subsequent additions to ditto.
	Interest charged on ditto.

Profit and Loss Account.

Dead Losses.	*Clear Gains.*
Trade Expenses : — Rent, rates, gas, fuel, wages, stamps, stationery, insurance, freight, repairs, advertisements, travelling expenses, carriage.	Discount ⎫ Interest . . ⎬ Allowed to me. Commission ⎭
Depreciation by wear and tear.	Rent paid me by sub-tenant.
Loss by death, fire, water, etc. ; Goods used as samples.	
Discount ⎫ Interest . . ⎬ I allow others or Commission ⎭ charge on capital.	
Bad Debts. Any *Reserve Fund.*	

Goods or Trade Account.

Buying Side.	*Selling Side.*
What bought for.	What sold for.
	Value at cost price of goods left unsold.

Credit Excesses are here in my favour, because these are my own accounts. The credit excess of Goods account is *Gross Profit;* the credit excess of P. & L. is *Net Profit;* the credit excess of Capital account is *Final Net Capital.* Each Excess is *carried up* to the same side of the account above it. None come into Balance Sheet. Final Net Capital = Initial Net Capital + Profits − Losses.

THE LEDGER ACCOUNTS.

THE SINGLE-ENTRY ACCOUNTS.

Those of my Banker, Cashier, Customers, etc. ; whose Debit Balances are Final Assets, and Credit Balances Final Liabilities, for *Final Balance Sheet.*

D.ᵣ   RECEIVING SIDE.   PAYING-AWAY SIDE.   C.ᵣ

Valuation Account.

| Business Premises, Trade Plant, Machinery, Horses and Vans, Office Furniture, Fixtures, Goods left unsold at close of Books. | Depreciation by wear and tear; loss by accident, theft, death, etc. ; or sale. |

Bank Account.

| What my Banker *receives* from me or for me. | What my Banker *pays away* to me or for me. |

Cash Account.

| What my Cashier *receives* for me. | What my Cashier *pays away* to me for me. |

Bills Receivable Account.

(*I receive first.*)

| The stamped written promises I *receive* from my Debtors instead of cash. | The stamped written promises I *give back* when I receive the promised cash. |

Bills Payable Account.

(*I pay away first.*)

| The stamped written promises I *receive* back from my Creditors when I pay the promised cash. | The stamped written promises I *give* my Creditors instead of giving cash. |

Smith's Account.

| What Smith *receives* from me. | What Smith *parts with* to me. |

Debit Balances are here in my favour, because these are others' accounts, and not my own. Every Debit Balance goes as an asset into Final Balance Sheet ; every Credit Balance as a Liability. Final Net Capital = Final Assets — Final Liabilities.

PROVING BOOKS.

PROVING BOOKS BY TRIAL BALANCE.

Showing Total Debits and Total Credits of every account after debiting Goods left unsold to Valuation account as an asset, and crediting Trade account with them as if sold.

Trial Balance.

	DEBITS.			CREDITS.	
Double-Entry accounts. My own accounts.	£100	Capital account	£500	Excess of *Credits* over Debits, *i.e.*, of Initial Capital + Profit over Losses = Final Net Capital, £580 (*d*).
	120	Profit and Loss account	—	
	600	Trade account	900	
Excess of *Debits* over Credits, *i.e.*, of Assets over Liabilities = Final Net (*c*) Capital, £580.	100	Valuation account ...	20	Single-Entry accounts: those of my Banker, Cashier, Customers, etc.
	480	Bank account	200	
	400	Cash account	360	
	100	Bills Receivable account	80	
	60	Bills Payable account ...	100	
	300	Personal accounts ...	100	
Grand Total Debits,	£2,260 (*a*)		(*b*) £2,260	Grand Total Credits.	

1st Proof . . Grand Totals (*a*) and (*b*) must be alike.

2nd Proof . . They must be the same as the *Journal* Debit Total and Credit Total.

3rd Proof . . The Excesses (*c*) and (*d*) must be alike; *i.e.*, the Excess of the *Credits* in the Double-Entry Set must be the same as the Excess of the *Debits* in the Single-Entry Set.

4th Proof . . Balancing and closing every account, and showing that the Balance of Capital account equals the Excess of Assets over Liabilities in Final Balance Sheet : *i.e.*, Initial Capital + Net Profit = Final Assets – Final Liabilities.

DOUBLE-ENTRY BOOKKEEPING.

THEORETICAL PART.

The Object of Bookkeeping.—The object of Book-keeping is to record our money transactions in such a way that we can readily tell at any time (1) what we are worth, (2) what net profits we are making, (3) what our customers owe us, and (4) what we owe them.

Double-Entry Bookkeeping is a device for detecting omissions and errors. Every transaction is entered twice over; it is recorded on opposite sides of two different accounts. When the totals of these two sides do not agree, we know something is wrong. If a Journal is kept, we have four totals which must be alike. And, without the Journal, we have always (1) two totals, and (2) two excesses, which must agree. Double Entry, then, is a device for testing or *proving our Books.*

Books Required.—The Journal and the Ledger are the principal books. All others are subsidiary.

1. The *Ledger* is the one indispensable book. From this we make out our customers' accounts. It is a complete picture of our business. Whatever other books

we keep, this must contain the substance of them all. Making entries in the Ledger we call "*posting.*" Understanding the Ledger is understanding the whole science and art of Bookkeeping.

2. The *Sales Book*, or *Day Book*, is for recording Credit Sales—Goods sold and not paid for at the time of sale. This and the Cash Book together show us what we sell our Goods for.

3. The *Invoice Book*, or *Purchases Book*, is for entering Credit purchases—Goods bought and not paid for at the time. This and the Cash Book together tell us what we have paid for our Goods. The invoices we receive when Goods are delivered, if filed together or gummed into a book, would form an Invoice Book.

4. The *Cash Book* is a record of money actually received, and money actually paid away. Bank notes count as money. When a Banking account is kept no other paper money is booked as cash.

5. The *Bank Pass Book* shows what my Banker receives from me, or for me. My cheques, when endorsed, show what he pays back to me, or to other people for me, at my request, on presenting a cheque or order signed by me.

6. The *Bills Receivable Book* records what stamped written promises of money I have received from my debtors, and when their money will be paid.

7. The *Bills Payable Book* records what stamped written promises of money I have given to my creditors, and when I must pay the money.

8. The *Waste Book* contains rough entries, made at the moment, to be afterwards transferred to other books.

9. The *Journal* is useful (1) as a help to posting, and (2) as an additional check; but is not necessary. It is used by wholesale houses very generally. It shows every transaction first as a Debit—*i.e.* on the debit side—of one account, then as a Credit—*i.e.* on the creditor side—of some other account.

Theory of Debtor and Creditor.—Debtor means *receiver*; creditor, *payer, one who parts with something.* The Dr. side of an account is that on which I enter what the man *whose name heads the account* receives from me. The Cr. side is that on which I enter what the man *whose name heads the account* pays to me, or parts with on my account. It must be carefully noticed that it is *the person whose name heads the account* that receives what is put on the Dr. side, and pays away to me what is put on the Cr. side; and the learner will have clearer ideas if he imagines every account to be a *personal* one. Bank account is Banker's account; Cash account is Cashier's account. Suppose my business large enough for me to employ a separate clerk for every separate account. One has charge of my Trade Plant, horses and vans, premises, etc.: we will call him Valuation clerk. He has charge of my *permanent assets*, the property I buy, not to sell again, but *to use in my business.* If I buy a horse for £60, my Cashier pays away the money, and puts £60 on the paying-away or credit side of his account; my Valuation clerk receives an addition to his stock of permanent assets, and writes £60 on the Dr. or receiving side of his account. When Smith sends me £10 to pay his account, Cashier receives £10, and writes it on the Dr. or receiving side of his account; Smith has paid away £10, and so £10 must be entered on the Cr. or paying-away side of Smith's account. One of my clerks, representing Smith, makes this entry for him. But as Smith's name heads the account, it is Smith's account, not mine. My own account, in my Ledger, is called Capital account, and is often headed with my name. The name must always be understood. If, when I begin business, I have £500 at the Bank, £200 at my shop, and Trade Plant worth £300, I must be supposed to hand over or pay away £500 to my Banker, £200 to my Cashier, and £300 to my Valuation clerk, at the outset. Each of these three clerks debits his own account with the value he has received—*i.e.* he writes it on the Debit or receiving side of his account. And as I, the master of the business, have paid it away, I write the total, £1000, on the Cr. or paying-away side of my own account. So with Bills—stamped written promises to pay money owing? When the clerk in charge of my Bills Receivable receives, instead of cash, a Bill Receivable, he enters it on the Dr. or receiving side of his account. When the promised money has been paid me, my clerk hands back the Bill, and writes its value on the Cr. or paying-away side, because he has paid away *the Bill.* When I pay away my own acceptance, my stamped written promise to pay £100, my Bills Payable clerk enters £100 on the Cr. side of his account, because he has *parted* with a Bill. When I keep my promise by paying, I get back my Bill Payable, and my clerk debits Bills Payable account £100, because he has received *a Bill.* The student must note carefully that it is *a Bill* for £100, not £100 cash that is received and therefore debited. The cash is Cashier's business, and must be *credited* to his account, because it is paid away by Cashier. So with Goods. The Goods clerk debits his account when he receives Goods, when Goods are bought; he credits it when Goods are parted with, whether sold, stolen, taken for use of proprietor, given away, or destroyed. Hence the buying side in a Goods account is the Dr. side; the selling side, Cr. Now, when Goods are sold for cash, Cashier receives and debits his account; Goods clerk parts with property in his charge and credits his account. On the other hand, when I buy Goods for cash, my Cashier pays away and credits his account; my Goods clerk receives and debits Goods account. If my pony worth £20 is killed, my Valuation clerk's account must be credited, for £20 worth has been parted with. If I draw out of my business £30 to live upon, Cashier pays it away to me, and credits his account £30; I receive it, and debit my own personal account, the Capital account, £30. The rule of Dr. and Cr., then, is "*Debit the receiver for what is received; credit the giver for what is parted with.*"

This seems simple enough. But, in order to provide a *double entry* for every transaction, we have to open in the Ledger a *fictitious account* called *Profit and Loss account*, and our rule will not help us in making entries in that account, unless we remember that Profit and Loss account (with all its subdivisions) is a part of MY OWN PERSONAL ACCOUNT, debit entries being against me, and credit entries in my favour; just as in other personal accounts debits are against the person whose name heads the account. If my van, worth £20, gets destroyed, my Valuation clerk credits his account £20, because £20 worth has gone out, or has been parted with, of the property in his charge. But which account must be debited? Who receives, by the accident? No one. I debit Profit and Loss account— *i.e.*, enter it in my own Personal account against me on Dr. side. When my Banker allows me £5 interest on my deposit account, I can either get the money, and Cashier will debit his account when he receives it, or the Banker's representative will debit Banker's account in my books, because the Banker is retaining £5 belonging to me ; he has *received* £5 value from me in the use of my money, and owes it to me. But what account must I credit? Who has paid away anything, or parted with anything? You may think the Banker has. But if I have debited the Banker £5, and now credit him with £5, one entry cancels the other and neither need have been made. If the Banker has not paid me the £5 it is clear that I must debit his account £5. This is a *clear gain*, a clear addition to my property without any money being spent on it. I credit it to Profit and Loss. This really means that I credit my own personal account with it. It is a clear gain—an addition to the capital I lent to my business at first, and being due to me must be credited to my account. Profit and Loss is a fictitious account, which receives *dead losses* on its Dr. side and *clear gains* on its Cr. side. Whenever money or money's worth goes out of my business *without anything tangible coming back to me for it*, it is a dead loss, and one entry for it must be made on the Dr. side of Profit and Loss. Whenever money comes into my business *over and above all that has been spent on the transaction,* that is a clear gain, and one entry of it must be on the Cr. side of Profit and Loss. This will be better understood after reading the article on Double Entry. If the Banker handed over to me the £5 cash for the use of my money, his account would receive no entry at all in my books, because the transaction neither increases nor lessens what the Banker owes me. It is one of many transactions which I need never book at all. It is opened and closed simultaneously, and needs no record, as between the Banker and me. But as between my *business* and me, it needs a record, for here is £5 profit to be credited to my personal account hereafter, if not swallowed up by losses. If I made out the Banker's account for this, I should debit him with the use of my money, and credit him with the £5 he has paid away, and both sides being equal, the account is opened and closed simultaneously, for the interest is not due till the day it is paid. The second rule for Dr. and Cr. then is, "*Debit dead losses; Credit clear gains.*"

Thus it must be distinctly understood that I must *not always* debit the receiver, and credit the giver or payer, at least not the *apparent* receiver or giver. The real receiver to be debited may be myself; the real giver to be credited may be myself. My own personal account is the one to be debited or credited in some cases. Many transactions are really double, involving four entries, if booked in full, as will be explained in detail under Double Entry. When I pay my landlord £20 rent, the landlord receives £20, but I do not debit his account £20 unless I have previously credited it £20. When I am paid £15 commission for selling goods for another merchant, that merchant pays away £15 to me, but I do not credit his account with £15 unless I have previously debited him as owing £15. This must be so for the simple reason that when I debit a man's account with £20, it shows that he has received £20 from me, and *owes me* £20, unless there is an entry on the other side which cancels it. By debiting the landlord's account with £20, I represent him as owing me £20; similarly by crediting the merchant's account with £15, I represent him as my creditor for £15, and myself as owing him £15 : both representations are false.   Mistakes of this kind are best avoided by remembering that in all the Single-Entry set of accounts, Debit Excesses are Assets of mine, representing money owing to me ; while Credit Excesses are Liabilities, representing money I owe. *The Credit side is that in favour of the person whose name heads the account ;* hence the expression "to his credit be it said," *i.e.,* in his favour. The Debit side is that *against* the person whose name heads the account, and the side in *my favour*, since what he owes me is an asset of mine.   This is the reason why in the Double-Entry set of accounts, of which the Profit and Loss account may be taken as the type, clear gains go on the Cr. side, for they are *my gains*, they are in my favour ; whereas dead losses are *against me*, they tend to lessen my original capital, and go on the Dr. side of Profit and Loss account.   That account is really a portion of my own Personal account, kept separate in order that we may see gains and losses more clearly.   Our booking would be quite correct, if, every time I get a bad debt, or lose a horse, I debit my Personal Capital account, instead of debiting Profit and Loss account. This is a lessening of capital, a lessening of what the business owes me, just as much as drawing out money for my private use, and that must be debited to my personal account because *received* back by me from the Cashier. So when a clear gain is made, what the business owes me will be increased, and my personal account must be credited with it, just as much as when I put more money into the business from a legacy left me. Then I pay it away to Cashier, who debits it to his account, and I credit my own personal account. And in the case of business gains, my Banker, my Cashier, or some of my clerks or customers, have collectively or singly these gains in their possession, and they are debited to their accounts just as surely ; and as they belong to me, they are credited to my personal account. Thus, viewing Profit and Loss account as part of my own personal account, the general rule holds good, " Debit the receiver ; Credit the giver." But a beginner will find it easier to say, " Debit dead losses ; Credit clear gains." " Debit assets ; Credit liabilities." " Credit initial net capital as a Liability the business owes me."

One side at a time must be considered in determining whether a transaction is to be entered on the Dr. or the Cr. side of an account. When I receive £5 from Anderson, I turn to Anderson's account, and ask, Does Anderson receive this from me, or does he pay it away to me ? As he pays it away, I write £5 on the Cr. side, and so make him my *creditor* for £5. I do this without looking across to the Dr. side. Possibly, I find £100 there. He owes me £100 less the £5 just booked, and is my debtor, not my creditor. When I balance his account I get the *combined effect*, the *resultant*, of all the entries on both sides. But in posting any single transaction, what I have to consider is whether it increases Anderson's indebtedness to me or the reverse; whether Anderson receives more from me, or pays me back a part.

How Differently the same Transaction is entered in Different People's Books.—It will help the learner in understanding the theory of Dr. and Cr. to notice how differently Brown and Jones book the same transaction, in which both are equally concerned. Jones sends Brown Goods invoiced at £4. As Jones has parted with Goods, he enters £4 on the Cr. or selling side of his Goods account. As Brown has received Goods from him, he opens an account for Brown, and debits him £4. He credits Goods account, and debits Brown's account. Brown, however, having bought Goods, enters £4 on the Dr., receiving, or buying side of Goods account; and opens an account for Jones, and credits it with £4. Brown debits Goods account, and credits Jones' account— the reverse of what Jones did.

Now consider what is done when I send £20 to the Bank. My name is Gregory. The Banker, on receiving the money, turns to an account in his Ledger headed Gregory, and *credits* it with £20, because Gregory has paid it away to him, and he owes it to Gregory. I turn to Banker's account in my books, and *debit* it £20, because the Banker has received £20 from me, and owes it me. I also credit Cashier's account, because it is paid away out of the money in his keeping. The Banker credits my accounts in his books; I debit Banker's account in my books.

TECHNICAL TERMS USED IN BOOK-KEEPING.

BEFORE studying the various accounts, and Double Entry, the learner must know the meaning of some of the technical terms employed. Others are given in the Glossary at the end.

Capital is the excess of Assets over Liabilities, the excess of what I have and have owing to me over what I owe. Its general form is Cash at Bank + Cash at Home + Goods on hand + Trade Plant + debts owing to me (including Bills Receivable) – debts I owe (including Bills Payable): e.g., if I have £1000 at Bank, £500 at office, Goods worth £200, Plant £100, and £200 is owing to me, and I owe £500, my Initial Net Capital is £1500.

My **Assets** are my property—what I already have, and what is owing *to* me.

My **Liabilities** are my debts, including money I owe on Bills.

An **Account** is a statement of property, or of transactions, written in two opposite parallel columns. The Dr. or left-hand column shows what is *received* by the person whose name heads the account; the Cr. side shows what

he has *paid away* or *parted with*. The Dr. side is against
the person whose name heads the account; the Cr. side
is in his favour. The Double-Entry Set of accounts (*e.g.*,
the Profit and Loss account) are *the personal accounts of
the owner of the Business*. The Dr. side shows his dead
losses, the Cr. side his clear gains. In every account, not
a personal account of the owner, a Debit Excess is an
Asset belonging to the owner; a Credit Excess a Liability
of his.

Balancing and Closing an Account means (1)
adding up both sides on a detached slip of paper; (2) subtracting the less from the greater to find the Excess or
Balance; (3) writing the difference as *an equalising entry*
on the deficient side of the Ledger; (4) adding up both
sides to see that they are equal; (5) ruling off the two
equal amounts by double lines; (6) bringing down the
Excess or Balance on the Excess side—*i.e.*, the side in
excess before both were made equal. Specimens are given
in the Practical Part. In the Double-Entry Set of accounts
(*e.g.*, Profit and Loss account), the excesses are not called
Balances, though really so. These excesses show gains
or losses, increases to Initial Net Capital, or diminutions
of it. Other excesses come into Final Balance Sheet.
They are Assets or Liabilities; Assets when Debit Balances,
Liabilities when Credit Balances. But none of the excesses of the Double-Entry Set of accounts come into
Final Balance Sheet, because they are neither Assets nor
Liabilities.

Balance means **Excess**. The word must never be
used to mean *deficiency*. *A Balance at my Banker's* means

a Balance in my favour: a Debit *Excess* in the Banker's account in my books, a Credit Excess in my account in the Banker's books. *An overdrawn account at the Bank* of £20 means that the Banker has obligingly paid away for me all the money he had of mine, and has lent me £20 besides to complete some payment for me. This is a Credit Balance in Banker's account in my books, *a Liability* of mine; but in my account in the Banker's books it is an Asset of his, a Debit Balance.

A Debit Balance means a Debit Excess. In my books, all Debit Balances are *Assets* of mine, except those of my own personal accounts where they show losses or bankruptcy—losses in the Goods account and the Profit and Loss accounts, bankruptcy in my own Personal or Capital account.

A Credit Balance is a Credit Excess, a Liability of mine in every account, except in my own personal accounts, where it shows clear gains or Final Net Capital which my business has belonging to me, or owes me. In these, Credit, Excesses are in my own favour, just as in other people's accounts in my books Credit Excesses are in favour of that person whose name heads the account, and *against me.*

An Equalising Entry is not a Balance, though called so. It is the Balance with its sign changed. It is *negative*, the Balance positive, or *vice versâ*. A Credit Equalising Entry shows a Debit Balance; a Debit Equalising Entry shows a Credit Balance. The true Balance or Excess is written on the Excess side below the double line, in readiness for a new account.

Journalising a Transaction is debiting it to one account, and crediting it to some other, debits coming first, and in chronological order.

Posting a Transaction is Entering it in the Ledger in the two accounts affected by it, on the Dr. side of one, on the Cr. side of the other. This is done from the Journal, but may be done from the Waste Book if no Journal is used. In the Ledger, every transaction relating to the same person, or the same property, is grouped together under the same heading, so that all the Credits in his favour and all the Debits against him are seen together for easy balancing; whereas in the Journal the arrangement is not personal, but chronological.

Opening the Ledger means writing out the headings of the various accounts, and posting under each the various items of the *Opening Balance Sheet—i.e.* debiting my Assets and crediting my Liabilities at commencement, and crediting my own personal account (Capital account) with Initial Net Capital, or Excess of Assets over Liabilities.

Closing the Ledger means balancing and closing every account in it, ready for drawing out a *Final Balance Sheet*, showing Assets and Liabilities at close, and the Excess of Assets over Liabilities at that time, or *Final Net Capital*, due to me.

Final Balance Sheet shows Debit Balances as Assets on the right-hand side, and Credit Balances as Liabilities on the left-hand side. If I have credited to my own personal account (Capital account), as due to me from the business, all the *Net Profit*, or addition, made to my Initial Net Capital since opening books, and so put it along with the commencing Capital also credited to it as a Liability due to me from the business, then, inasmuch as that net profit is the excess of Assets over Liabilities when profits are not booked as a Liability, *the Assets will just equal the Liabilities* when net profit is credited to me as a Liability the business owes me. But, if I have left my Ledger open, and credited my own personal account with nothing but initial net capital, with nothing but what I lent the business at start, then the excess of Assets over Liabilities at close, *since there was no such excess at commencement*, must be just the same as net profit made in the interim. If it is not, our Books *prove wrong*. The learner cannot too carefully note that *none of the Profit and Loss accounts, nor any of the Goods or Trade accounts, send their excesses into Final Balance Sheet.* These accounts are really parts of my own personal account. Their Credit, Excesses, so far from showing Liabilities, show clear *gains.* Their Debit Excesses, so far from being Assets of mine, are *dead losses,* implying diminution of what I commenced business with. The only exception is the balance of Goods left unsold, which will be explained later on.

Taking out a Trial Balance is finding separately the total debits, then the total credits of every account in the Ledger; then the grand total of all the debits of all the accounts collectively, also the grand total of all the credits collectively. As every debit has a corresponding credit in some other account in the Ledger, and *vice versâ,* the grand total of debits must just equal the grand total of credits. And as the Ledger contains just the same items as the Journal, only differently arranged, these two totals in the Ledger Trial Balance must agree with the totals in the Journal. *Books prove wrong if these four totals are not exactly alike.*

I am *solvent* when my Assets at least equal my Liabilities; *insolvent* when Assets are less than Liabilities.

I *compound with my Creditors*, or make a *composition*, when they agree to accept a part only of what I owe them, say 16∴ 8*d.* in the £, as *a final settlement of the whole debt.*

DOUBLE ENTRY AND METHODS OF PROVING BOOKS.

EVERY transaction concerns two parties, and requires an entry in two different accounts—on the Dr. side of one, on the Cr. side of some other, an equal amount in both cases. Every debit has its corresponding credit; every credit its corresponding debit. Sometimes a number of debits in different accounts taken collectively correspond to one single credit in another. Then the *total* of all the debits must be the same as the single credit. Thus Jones may pay me a cheque for £20, £10 cash, and his acceptance for £70. As my Banker receives £20, my Cashier £10, and my Bills Receivable Clerk £70 as a stamped written promise, each debits his own account with the amount he receives; and Jones, having paid away £100, must be credited with the total £100. Sometimes several credits in different accounts all taken together have their double in a single debit in another account, equal to them all. If I buy Goods for £10 cash, more Goods for a cheque value £30, a third lot invoiced at £100, for which I give my own acceptance for £100, and a fourth lot invoiced at £60 of Roberts on credit, I have bought Goods for £200, and must enter that amount on the Dr. or buying side of Goods account. This is one side of the Ledger. On the other, Cashier must credit his account £10, for he has paid it away; the Banker will pay away £30 of my money when the cheque is presented, so Banker's account must be credited £30; Bills Payable Clerk will pay away a bill with my name across its face, and credit his account £100; lastly, Roberts' account must be credited with £60, for Roberts has paid away that value to me and I owe him for it. Hence, there are a number of credits amounting to £200, corresponding to a single debit of £200.

But there are transactions which, when booked fully, are *double transactions*, and involve *four entries*, two of which, a debit and a credit, are cancelled, and need never be entered. Several of these will be reasoned upon in the article on Fictitious Accounts, and others in that upon Omitted Entries. In some others, too, learners often debit or credit *the wrong person*. For instance, suppose I miss from my shop a case of cigars worth £10, and can hear nothing of them. What entry must I make? The property in charge of my Goods Clerk is lessened just as much as if I had sold the cigars. They have been parted with, and so Goods account must be credited £10. Who has received them? We must debit him, must we

T. P. 2

not? Yes, if we know the thief, and can get back our
£10 from him. But we cannot debit an unknown man,
nor is it any good to debit a· man who will never pay,
even if we know the thief. For a debit, unless cancelled
by an equal credit, implies *an Asset*—money to come into
my pocket. This transaction, so far from bringing money
into my pocket, has lessened what I had. It is a *dead
loss*, money's worth gone out, and nothing whatever back
in its place; and as it lessens my property, I debit *my
own personal account*. I put it along with dead losses on
the Dr. side of Profit and Loss account. If my uncle
leaves me a legacy of £300, and I put it into my business
as additional Capital, how must I post that? Who has
received? My Cashier, who has charge of the money.
He debits his account. Who has paid it away? I have
paid it to him. I credit my own Personal or Capital
account. A learner might argue that, as the uncle paid
it, or his executors did for him, he must be credited;
and as I received it, my Personal account must be debited.
To show the absurdity of this, open an account for my
uncle's executors, and credit it with £300; and debit
my own Personal or Capital account £300, and see what
those two entries mean. The credit entry in the account
headed "The Executors of my Uncle" means that I owe
them £300! The debit entry in my own Personal or
Capital account means that I have withdrawn £300 from
my capital, or, at all events, lessened by £300 what I put
into the business! My books would indicate that, instead
of being £300 better off for the legacy, I am £300 poorer,
which is absurd. The gift of my uncle is outside the

business entirely. It is only when I pay it over to the Cashier that it comes into my books.

We must also give a double entry to our *opening Balance Sheet*, or what we have and what we owe on reopening our books or commencing business. The cash I have has been received by Cashier and appeared as a Debit Balance in his last account; so of every other asset. Every opening asset must be debited; it was a Debit Excess when the account was closed. Every liability was a Credit Excess, and must be credited—*i.e.*, placed on the side in favour of the creditor whose name heads the account. If, at commencement, I have £300 at Bank, I debit Bank account £300; if £100 cash, I debit Cash account £100; if Goods worth £80, I debit Goods account £80; if Trade Plant worth £20, I debit Valuation account £20; if Richards owes me £200, I debit Richards' account £200; if I owe Roberts £400, I *credit* Roberts' account £400. Subtracting Liabilities from Assets, my Initial Net Capital is £300. I am worth £300 at commencement. This I have *paid away* to my various clerks, some to the Banker, some to the Cashier, and so on: I must therefore *credit* my own account with £300. The business owes me £300. I open an account at the end of the personal accounts, put my own name at the head of it, and credit it with £300, just as I should credit a customer who lent £300 to my business.

If, then, we never make a debit without a corresponding credit, and never a credit without a corresponding debit, and if we enter the same money in both cases, it follows that the grand total of the *debits* of all the accounts taken collectively must exactly equal the grand total of the *credits* of all the accounts taken collectively. This is the first test of correct books :—

Is the grand total of all the debits in the Ledger equal to the grand total of all the credits in the Ledger ?

A second test is afforded by the agreement or disagreement of two *excesses*. On opening my books, if I credit to my own personal account my initial net Capital, entering it as a Liability the business owes me, the business owes me all the excess of my Assets over my Liabilities at that time; and when I have credited that as a Liability, there is no longer any excess; *Assets and Liabilities are just equal.* For instance, if my Assets exceed my Liabilities by £300 at commencement, and I increase those Liabilities by £300, by entering what the business owes me as a Liability, there is then no excess of Assets over Liabilities. The business begins with nothing, for it owes to me all it has. It is not in debt; it can just pay me, and nothing over. As, therefore, it begins just solvent, and no more, if at the end of a month I find the Assets exceed the Liabilities by £80 (say), I know the business has made £80 net profit during the month. But among my accounts in the Ledger there is one, or more, where all clear profits and all dead losses are recorded, and the excess of clear gains (or additions to what the business owns) over losses is written as net profit or increase. This is the Profit and Loss account and its subdivisions. The profit on the Goods or Trade account is, of course, included in the gains. The net gain, as seen in Profit and Loss account, must, of course, agree with the

increase of Assets over Liabilities. They were equal at
the beginning of the month; now Assets are in excess by
£80. If Profit and Loss account does not also show a
clear or net gain of £80, a credit excess of £80, £80
more gains than losses, our books are wrong. The second
test of correct books, then, is this :—

*Does the Net Profit as shown in Profit and Loss account
agree with the increased excess of Assets over Liabilities as
shown in the other accounts ?*

The rule of Double Entry is so completely carried out,
that it is applied to the *equalising entries* made in balancing
and closing the accounts in the Ledger. This will be
explained under " Journalising the Closing Entries."

Practical Rules for Posting.

1. In opening Balance Sheet, debit Assets, credit Liabilities, and credit Capital account or Owner's personal
account with the *excess* of Assets over Liabilities (net
Capital).

2. Ask " Who *receives* this ? " Debit the receiver with
what is received; but *never* unless the entry represents an
Asset to come into the pocket of the owner of the business,
unless cancelled by a credit entry.

3. Ask " Who *pays away* this, who *parts with* this to
me ? " Credit the payer with what he parts with; but
never unless the entry represents a *Liability* of the Owner
of the business, a debt he will have to pay, if not paid
beforehand, as shown by a debit entry in that account.

4. If it is not easy to say *who receives*, or *who parts
with* the value, suspect the receiver or the payer to be
the owner of the business. It is probably a clear gain or

a dead loss to the owner. It is an item for Profit and Loss account. *Debit dead losses ; credit clear gains.* The two parties concerned in such transactions are (1) my business considered apart from myself, and (2) myself. What other parties give or receive does not come into my books.

5. Remember that *the Dr. side in Trade account is the buying side.* When I buy for Cash, Cash goes out and is credited, Goods come in and are debited.

Classification of the Ledger Accounts.—They are often divided into three classes :—

1. Real or Property accounts—as (1) Cash account, (2) Bank account, (3) Goods account, (4) Valuation account (including all *permanent* Assets like premises, trade plant, horses and vans, and machinery), (5) Bills account. Bills, like Bank notes, *represent* real property.

2. Personal accounts, showing what my customers owe me, and what I owe them. A Bill, when dishonoured, is debited to the personal account of the defaulter but is not treated as personal till mature.

3. Nominal or Fictitious accounts, being those opened in order to provide a double entry for every transaction and for every important fact connected with my business. They all relate to Initial Capital, or what increases or lessens it, viz., profits and losses ; or to Final Net Capital, being Assets minus Liabilities. They are (1) Capital account, (2) Profit and Loss account, and (3) Balance account (*i.e.* Balance Sheet reversed, showing Assets as Debit Excesses on its debit side, and Liabilities as Credit Excesses on its Credit side).

Objections to this Classification.

(1) The Nominal or Fictitious accounts represent real property as much as the Real accounts. They contain the "doubles" or second entries of the very items given in detail in those accounts.

(2) The Nominal or Fictitious accounts are really the *personal accounts* of the owner of the business. Capital account is his own personal account; he is credited with what he lends to the business. Profit and Loss account is a part of his own personal account; it is credited with all additions to Capital (gains), and debited with all lessenings of Capital (losses). Net gain, the Credit excess of Profit and Loss account, is credited ultimately to the owner's personal account to increase Initial Capital; for the gain belongs to him. The Balance Account is a mere collection of Assets and Liabilities at close, and represents real property.

(3) Goods or Trade account, too, belongs to the owner's *personal* account, for its credit excess shows how much more is got for the Goods than is spent upon them, and this clear gain goes with other gains to the Cr. side of Profit and Loss; and ultimately to the Cr. side of owner's Personal or Capital account. It is true, however, that the balance of Goods left unsold goes as an Asset with the Real account assets.

(4) From one point of view, every account in the Ledger is *a personal* account.

The natural classification of accounts into (1) other people's accounts, (2) the owner's own personal accounts. Accounts naturally divide themselves into two Sets.

1. *The Single-Entry Set of Accounts*, whose Debit Balances are *Assets*, and whose credit Balances are *Liabilities*, for Final Balance Sheet.   They include the accounts for Valuation, Bank, Cash, Petty Cash, Bills, and all personal accounts, *except the Capital account, and the other personal accounts of the owner of the business.*

2. *The Double-Entry Set of Accounts*, those not used in Single-Entry Bookkeeping, being *the personal accounts of the owner of the business.*   They are Capital account, Profit and Loss account, and Goods or Trade account. *They all relate to Capital, or to increase or to diminution of Capital.*

The Single-Entry Set are the accounts of my clerks or of my customers (Valuation Clerk, Cashier, Banker, etc.).

The Double-Entry Set are *my own* accounts, considering myself apart from my business.

THE SINGLE-ENTRY SET OF ACCOUNTS.

How we find out what we are worth from the Single-Entry Set.

THESE are the only accounts used in Single-Entry Book-keeping.   They show us our Assets on the Dr. side, and our Liabilities on the Cr. side ; and the Debit Excess at close of Books is Final Net Capital, or what we are then worth.

Valuation Account.—Let us suppose a merchant opening a new Ledger with a new year.   Some of his property consists of *permanent assets*, property not to sell, but to keep and use in his business. One of his clerks, whom we will call Valuation Clerk, has these in his charge, opens an account for them, and enters on the Dr. or receiving side the value of the fixtures, trade plant, business premises, horses and vans, and any other permanent assets belonging to the firm on January 1st. If, during the year, any addition is made to them—if any new premises are erected, a fresh horse bought, any permanent improvements made to premises, adding to their value, should a vessel be purchased, or a lease of premises bought—the value of all these would also be entered on the Debit or receiving side. On the other hand, if a horse got killed, a van destroyed, an uninsured or insured warehouse burnt, an uninsured or insured ship wrecked, all these would lessen the value of the permanent assets in the Valuation Clerk's charge, and are entered on the Cr. or parting-with side. At the end of the year, too, it is customary to write off a percentage for depreciation by wear and tear. Premises worth £800 in January may be worth but £720 in December. So, too, with most of the other permanent assets. The amount written off or deducted for depreciation must go on the Cr. side, because it is value *parted with*; it is a lessening of the Asset recorded on the Dr. side. When Valuation Clerk's account is balanced on December 31st, its *Debit Balance* is one of the Final Assets to come into Final Balance Sheet.

Bank Account.—Some of the merchant's property is money lodged with his Banker. His Banker's account in his books shows on the Dr. side what the *Banker* has received from him, and any increases to his deposits from interest for the use of his money. On the Cr. side are entered all amounts withdrawn. The *Debit Balance*, the excess of what the Banker receives from him over what he pays away to him, or for him, shows what he has still belonging to him. It is one of the Assets for Final Balance Sheet.

Cash Account is Cashier's Account.—All the moneys received by Cashier are entered on the Debit side; all sums paid away by him on the Cr. side. The *Debit Balance*, the excess of what he has received over what he has paid away, is what he still has. That is another Asset for Final Balance Sheet. The Cashier owes it to the merchant.

Bills Receivable Account, the account of the clerk who receives and pays away the stamped written promises to pay money owing to the merchant.—They are paper money, and coming in instead of cash, are first entered on the Dr. or receiving side. They represent money, and *are considered as payment* until the time named on them. When the money promised on them has been paid by the Acceptor who has signed them, the Bill is given back to him, and the Bills Receivable Clerk, *having parted with a bill*, enters its value on the Cr. or paying-away side. This Credit entry neutralises the Asset on the Debit side. It no longer exists as a Bill but as Cash, and appears on the Dr. side of Cash account instead of the Dr. side of Bills Receivable account. If it is dishonoured by not being paid when the time comes, the Credit entry is made in the Bills Receivable account, though the Bill is not parted with, much the same as if honoured and given back to Acceptor. This is done, because the *Asset no longer exists as a Bill.* The debt, however, is still owing, and becomes then *a personal* one. An account is opened for the defaulter, the dishonoured acceptor, and he is debited with the amount. The Asset disappears from Bills Receivable account, but reappears in the Personal account. If at the end of the year there is a *Debit Excess* in Bills Receivable account, say of £80, it means that the Clerk still holds a Bill or Bills for £80 not yet mature. This is one of the merchant's Assets for Final Balance Sheet.

Bills Payable Account, the account of the clerk who has charge of the stamped written promises made by the merchant to his creditors. They all represent money *he owes*—they are *Liabilities*; and as they are paid away as paper money, the clerk enters them on the Cr. or paying-away side of Bills Payable account. They are kept by the merchant's *creditors,* to be presented for payment when mature. When honoured the clerk receives back the Bill, and the Liability no longer existing, it is cancelled by a debit entry. The Liability appears in Cashier's account, or Banker's account, instead of Bills Payable account. If, at the end of the year, there are any Bills out not yet mature—*i.e.* if there is a *Credit Balance* in Bills Payable account, it is a Liability for Final Balance Sheet. The merchant owes that sum on Bills out against him.

Personal Accounts.—The merchant may also owe money to creditors for Goods he has bought, and some

of his customers may owe him for Goods they have received
from him. These form Personal accounts. An account
is opened for each debtor and for each creditor. It is
headed with the person's name—say Robert Glover. If
Robert Glover owes the merchant £200, his account is
debited £200; he has received £200 worth from the
firm, and still owes it. If Thomas Webb has parted with
£80 worth to the firm, and has not yet been paid, his
account is *credited* with £80. If the merchant has mortgaged his premises—*i.e.* borrowed money on them, he opens
a Mortgagee's account, and *credits* that account with £700,
if that amount has been lent to him. It must be carefully
noted (1) that it is *the person whose name heads the account*
who receives what is put on the Dr. side, and who pays
away what is put on the Cr. side; and (2) that opening
Assets are debited, and opening *Liabilities credited*. A
Debit Balance shows that that person has *received* from
the merchant more than he has paid back, and *owes* that
amount to him; a Credit Balance shows that the person
whose name heads the account has parted with to him
more than he has received from him, and the Balance is
due to that person. *The Credit side is that in favour of
the person whose name heads the account*; the Debit side
is the side against him, the side in favour of the merchant.
Debit Balances are his Assets, Credit Balances his Liabilities.
The Debit Excesses show amounts owing to him, the Credit
Excesses show amounts which he owes to others. This is
the distinguishing mark of all the accounts belonging to
the Single-Entry Set—that Debit Balances are Owner's
Assets.

If, then, at the year's end, we collect together all the Debit Balances found in any of this set of accounts, and put them on one side of *a Summary account*, and place all the Credit Balances on the other side, and find the Excess of the Debits over the Credits, we have the Excess of Final Assets over Final Liabilities, which is the Merchant's Final Net Capital, or *what he is worth at close of Books*. Such a Summary account is called a *Final Balance Sheet* when the Assets are placed to the right and Liabilities to the left; but *a Balance Account* when Debit Balances are taken to the Debit side as Assets, and Credit Balances to the Credit side as Liabilities. This is just what we do when we balance and close the Single-Entry Set of accounts.

But we can arrive at this final result another way, by *Trial Balance*, without closing any one of the accounts. For if we find the sum of all the Debits throughout this set of accounts, and then the sum of all the Credits, the Excess of the Debits over the Credits, taking the whole set together, is the Excess of Assets over Liabilities, or Final Net Capital.

Excesses or Balances in the Single-Entry Set of Accounts.

In Valuation account, Cash account, and Bills Receivable account, when there is any Excess or Balance at all, it must be *a Debit Balance* or Asset. For in Valuation account, the Credit side, which shows depreciation, loss, damage or other lessening of the Asset on the Debit side, can never show a sum greater than the whole original value of the property. In Cash account, Cashier can never pay away more cash than he has first received and debited. In Bills Receivable account, the entries on the Credit side are not made till the Acceptances have matured, and been either discounted, honoured, oɪ dishonoured; till the Asset, entered on the Debit side when the Bill is received, has ceased to exist as a Bill. The amount credited as honoured or dishonoured may equal, but can never exceed, the amount debited as promised.

In Bank account, too, any Balance must be a Debit Balance or Asset, except in the rare case when a Banker obliges a good customer by allowing him *to overdraw his account*, and get into his debt. An overdrawn Balance at Bank means money owing to the Banker—a Liability of the merchant's.

In Bills Payable account, any Balance must be a *Credit* Balance, a Liability, a Bill not yet mature. For Bills Payable are first paid away to one's creditors, and appear first on the Credit side. When mature, honoured or dishonoured, entries are made on the Dr. side, to cancel the Liability on the Cr. side. But Bills cannot be presented to us for payment for a greater sum than we have given our creditors Bills for.

When, therefore, we speak of a Cash Balance, a Bank Balance, Valuation Balance, Bills Receivable Balance, we are speaking of Debit Balances or Assets.

But a Bills *Payable* Balance must be a Liability or Credit Balance. An *overdrawn Balance at Banker's* is also a Liability or Credit Excess.

A Reserve Fund Balance, too, must be what remains of a Liability. (See article on "Reserve Fund and Mortgage Account.")

THE DOUBLE-ENTRY SET OF ACCOUNTS.
The Fictitious Accounts.

THESE accounts are not used in Single-Entry Book-keeping. They are Capital account, Profit and Loss account, and Trade or Goods account, with all the sub-divisions of each of them. Without these, we could not find "a double" for many of the entries made in the Single-Entry Set. The Double-Entry Set represents essentially the same facts, and leads to the same final result as the Single-Entry Set; but the point of view is totally different, and the mode of getting at the result altogether unlike. With the exception of a few unimportant transactions not affecting the final result, every item and every transaction entered in any one of the Single-Entry accounts is entered again in one or other of the Double-Entry Set, but always *on opposite sides of the Ledger.* And why on opposite sides? Because all the Double-Entry accounts are really *the owner's own personal accounts*; whereas the Single-Entry accounts are none of them his own accounts, but his Banker's account, his Cashier's account, etc. And what appears in these latter accounts, as debits owing by them to him, appear in the Double-Entry accounts as credits, value handed over by him to them, and so credited to him. On the other hand, in the Single-Entry Set, credits represent what is owing by him to the person whose name heads the account. These being debts of the owner, are debited to his personal account : *i.e.*, the same facts are represented in the two sets of accounts in an exactly opposite manner ; debits in the one set appear as credits in the other, credits in the one as debits in the other.

If, at commencement, I have Trade Plant worth £80, £500 at Bank, £200 at shop, hold a Bill for £320, and Prior owes me £300, all these being Assets in my favour, but in the possession of various clerks who have received them from me, will be debited to their several accounts in the Single-Entry accounts, but credited to my own Personal or Capital account for the total, £1400. If there is an outstanding Bill against me (a Bill Payable) for £400, and I owe Rogers £250, these being Liabilities of mine are put on the Cr. side of the Single-Entry accounts, but on the Debit side of my own Personal or Capital account, because I owe £650, and so must debit myself £650. If, at any time, I add £400 to my Capital, my Cashier receives it and debits his account £400 ; I credit my own Personal or Capital account £400, because the money is mine, and I have paid it away to Cashier for use in the business.

Here, again, a debit in a Single-Entry account is identical with a credit in a Double-Entry account. Another way of expressing the same fact is this :—" In the Double-Entry accounts the side in my own favour is the *Credit* side, as in all personal accounts the Cr. side is that in favour of the person whose name heads the account. In the Single-Entry accounts the side in my own favour is the *Debit* side, that being the side against the person whose name heads the account; and none of these accounts are my c·wn."

Another characteristic of the Double-Entry Set of accounts is that they all relate to *Capital* or to increase or lessening of Capital—*i.e.* Profits and Losses; whereas the Single-Entry Set all relate to Assets and Liabilities, to what I have or have owing to me, and what I owe. One Set views in the *abstract* what the other shows in the *concrete* form.

The learner may find, in some books, the word "Stock" used for Capital. In other books "Stock account" means Goods or Trade account, not Capital account. He must distinguish one from the other.

How to find out what I am worth from the Double-Entry Set of Accounts.

If, on beginning trade, I fold a piece of paper lengthwise down the middle, and on the right-hand side enter what I have to begin with (my *Initial Net Capital*), and on the same side put down every *clear gain* I make—*i.e.* every amount that comes into my business without anything whatever going out to procure it; and if also I add, on the same side, my *Trade Profit*, the excess of what I get for my Goods over what I give for them; then, on adding, I have what I am now worth, my *Final Net Capital*, unless I have incurred some *dead losses* by having to pay away money without getting back anything whatever that is tangible or saleable in return. But I have, in fact, suffered

T. P.

3

many of these losses or diminutions of Capital. I have paid away money as rent to the landlord, as rates and taxes to the collector, as salary to clerk, wages to office boy, for fire insurance, advertisements, stamps and stationery; a horse may have died, a debtor owing me £50 may have absconded, I may have had to pay interest on a mortgage or loan, and allow my customers discount for prompt payment. Any such losses I enter on the left-hand or debit side as *lessenings of Capital.* The difference between the two sides is the excess of Initial Net Capital *plus* clear profit made since, over dead losses suffered since; and this must be what I am now worth—my *Final Net Capital.*

This is a very different way of finding out what I am worth from the plan pursued in the Single-Entry Set of accounts. There the accounts are not my own, but my Clerks', my Banker's, or my Customers' accounts. On the debit side, throughout the whole Set, I enter what they *receive* from me, or from others for me; this is all *mine,* my Assets. On the Cr. side I enter every value *paid away* by them to me, or for me; this I owe them for: it is a Liability of mine. And the excess of what is mine over what I owe them for is the excess of Final Assets over Final Liabilities, and is what I am now worth; it is my Final Net Capital.

In the Double-Entry Set, then—

Final Net Capital = Initial Net Capital + Clear Profits — Dead Losses. (*a*)

In the Single-Entry Set—

Final Net Capital = Assets — Liabilities. (*b*)

(*a*) and (*b*) must be identical, whether positive or negative.

PROVING BOOKS.

SINCE the excess of Assets over Liabilities must be just the same as the excess of Initial Net Capital *plus* Clear Profits over Dead Losses, if these two excesses (the final results arrived at on closing the two Sets of accounts) do not exactly agree, we know there is error in our booking. Books prove correct, so far as final result is concerned, when *the Excess of all the Debits* over all the Credits in the Single-Entry Set just equals *the Excess of all the Credits* over all the Debits in the Double-Entry Set. Another way of putting it is to say that Final Net Capital as seen in Capital account, and obtained by adding to commencing Capital all clear gains and subtracting all dead losses, must agree with Final Net Capital as seen in Final Balance Sheet, and obtained by deducting Final Liabilities from Final Assets.

BALANCING AND CLOSING THE DOUBLE-ENTRY ACCOUNTS.

As it is desirable to keep profits and losses by themselves, apart from original Capital, and desirable also to keep by themselves what I spend on my Goods and what I get back for them when sold, we always want three Double-Entry accounts—*Capital account, Profit and Loss account,* and *Trade account.*` And the beginner should always open the Ledger with these three accounts, and always *in this fixed order,* because he can carry the credit excess of Trade account (the profit) to the credit side of Profit and

Loss account just above it, and add it to the other clear gains; and on balancing Profit and Loss account, he can carry the excess of gains over losses, *i.e.* the *Net* Profits, the credit excess of Profit and Loss account, to the credit side of Capital account just above it, to increase original Capital, and give us Final Net Capital. When these accounts are scattered about the Ledger, mixed up with those of the Single-Entry Set, the beginner has more trouble in transferring the Excesses, and is less likely to understand the *rationale* of proving Books, and seeing why the Balances of the Single-Entry Set are taken into Final Balance Sheet, whereas the Excesses (usually Credit Excesses) of the Double-Entry accounts are carried away to increase or diminish original Capital. It is desirable, at first, to separate the two Sets by a bold double line drawn all across the Ledger, so that the student may never have to hesitate about what he has to do with the Balance or Excess of any account, whether to carry it up, or take it away to Balance account or Balance Sheet.

Balances in Single-Entry Accounts; Excesses in Double-Entry Accounts.

In Practical Bookkeeping, the great difference between the two Sets of accounts is that every one of the Single-Entry accounts sends its Debit Balance as Asset, or its Credit Balance as Liability, into Final Balance Sheet; whereas not one of the Double-Entry Set does. (The Debit Balance of Goods on hand left unsold is the one solitary exception, and is treated later on.) Hence it is usual not to call any excesses Balances, except those of Single-Entry accounts. So we speak of the Credit *Excess* of Goods account, of the Credit *Excess* of Profit and Loss account, because these excesses do not come into Final Balance Sheet. But they are, in fact, balances increasing Initial Capital.

In closing the Double-Entry accounts, *we begin with Trade Account.* Its Credit Excess shows how much more we get for our goods when selling them than we gave for them when buying. The beginner will do well to mark the Dr. side the buying side, and the Cr. side the selling side. The Credit Excess is *Gross Profit,* increase to initial or original capital. This must go with other clear profits on the credit side of Profit and Loss account. This account is nothing but a collection of dead losses on its debit side and clear gains on its credit side. Its Credit Excess is *Net Profit,* or Increase to Capital, the excess of gains over losses. This must go on the Credit side of Capital account, to increase original Capital. Capital account is my own personal account, and receives from Profit and Loss account its Credit Excess as addition to the Initial Capital entered on its credit side when books were opened. Any additions made to Capital by fresh amounts invested in the business, by interest charged on Capital as a first claim on profits, go on its Cr. side as *adding* to Capital. On its Dr. side I enter all amounts withdrawn for private use not connected with the business, and the value of Goods taken out of stock for private consumption: these *lessen* original Capital. When

balanced, the Credit Excess shows Final Net Capital—
what I am worth when books are closed.

In the above reasoning, we have assumed a normal
business where *profits* are made, and both at commencement and at close the proprietor is solvent. There is a
Credit Excess in Goods account, showing a profit made on
Sales.   There is a *Credit Excess* in Profit and Loss account
after the profit on Goods has been credited to it, and
this shows an excess of Gains over Losses, a Net Profit.
In Capital account, after Net Gains have been credited
to it, there is a *Credit Excess* showing Final Net Capital.
But our method and reasoning are equally true when there
is no Capital at commencement, or even a Negative Capital
or Deficit; when the trader begins with borrowed money,
and incurs losses in business, ending in insolvency; when
he is insolvent to begin with, and becomes more and
more so.   If I begin business with £800 borrowed from
Yarnold, I am not insolvent, but simply have capital Nil.
In my Capital account I credit myself with Capital Nil;
in the Single-Entry Set I debit cash and credit Yarnold,
and my asset just equals my Liability: the Asset or Debit
is £800, the Liability or Credit £800.   But if, at commencement, my Assets are worth £800 and my Liabilities
amount to £1000, I am insolvent, and my capital must
go as a *Deficit* on the *Dr.* side of Capital account.   And
if I am unsuccessful in trade, and get less for my Goods
than I give for them, there will be a *Debit Excess* in Trade
account showing a Gross Loss.   And if, when this loss is
put with other losses, on the Dr. side of Profit and Loss
account, the losses more than swallow up any gains, there

will be a Debit Excess in Profit and Loss account, showing a *Net Loss*. And, when this Net Loss has been taken to the Debit side of Capital account, it increases the original Deficit and shows that I am more insolvent than ever. In the Double-Entry accounts, then, Excesses may be either Debit or Credit Excesses, but *Credit Excesses are the rule*. Debit Excesses show losses ; in Capital account insolvency. When there is a Debit Excess in Capital account, the Excess of Assets over Liabilities is a negative quantity. There is no excess at all, but a deficiency. There is still the same correspondence between the Double-Entry Set and the Single-Entry Set. Both show the same final result—a negative one. It is an excess of *Debits* in the Double-Entry Set and an excess of Credits in the Single-Entry Set ; whereas, in most Ledgers, the *Credits* are in excess in the Double-Entry Set, and the Debits in the Single-Entry Set.

The Double-Entry Set of Accounts in the Trial Balance.

Since the Credit Excess of Trade account is taken to the Credit side of Profit and Loss account, and the Credit Excess of Profit and Loss to the Credit side of Capital account, we may regard the entire Set of accounts as *the Owner's Personal account*, and treat the whole of them as one account. In arranging their totals in Trial Balance, it is best to separate them ftom the Single-Entry Set by a line drawn across the page, and see whether the Credits are as much in excess in this Set as the Debits

are in excess in the Single-Entry Set. The dividing
line must be disregarded in finding the Grand Totals of
both Sets.

The Unique Double Character of Goods or Trade Account.

We have placed this account among the Double-Entry
Set, because its Credit Excess ultimately reaches Capital
account, after passing through Profit and Loss account. It
is certainly part of *the Owner's own Personal account* in the
Ledger. But *it really belongs to both Sets*; and, except
in the rare case when stock of Goods is entirely sold or
burnt out, so that we have no Goods on hand left unsold,
it has *two balances*, or, more strictly, *a Balance and an
Excess*—a Balance to go as an Asset with the Single-Entry
Set, and a Credit Excess for the Credit side of Profit and
Loss account. This is true of no other account but of
Trade account, and its numerous subdivisions or subsidiary
accounts, such as Consignment Outwards, Contracts, Joint
Ventures, Ship account, etc. Goods left on hand unsold
at the time of closing books form one of my Final Assets,
and must come into Final Balance Sheet. As an Asset
they must be debited to some account among the Single-
Entry Set, either in an account to themselves or in Valuation Clerk's account. They must also be *credited to Goods
account as if sold*; otherwise we cannot calculate the Gross
Profit on Trade. If I bought four knives at 2s. I should
lay out 8s.; if I sold three of them at 2s. 6d. I should get
7s. 6d. only, but I should not lose, because I have a knife

worth 2s. remaining—worth 2s. at *Cost* price. To get at my
profit I add the 2s. to the 7s. 6d., and then find I have
gained 1s. 6d. ; for I have the other knife on hand. In
Trial Balances, as seen in most books, Goods on hand at
close are not included, because when accounts are not
balanced and closed, this entry, being Goods Debit Balance,
is not wanted any more than any other balance, and must
only be pencilled and not inked in. But it very much
assists a beginner in understanding Trial Balance and
getting out the final results from it, to include the Value
of Goods on hand among the Credits of Trade account,
and among the Debits of Valuation account. Trial
Balance then presents as complete a presentment of the
Owner's affairs as actually balancing and closing the Ledger
does. This method is pursued throughout the Practical
Part, and is strongly recommended to learners. So also is
that of separating the Ledger accounts into two Sets, and
of making them follow in the same fixed order. But it
must be noted that Goods on hand, debited to *Valuation*
account as a Final Asset in Final Balance Sheet, must
be debited to *Goods* account in posting Opening Balance
Sheet in next month's Ledger.

How the Valuation of Goods on hand at close can be found from the QUANTITIES Bought and Sold.

In actual business, the valuation is found by "stock-
taking." In examination papers it is usually given at the
end of the exercise, but sometimes inserted among the

directions, as if to tempt the unwary to overlook it altogether. It should always be journalised as a transaction;
as if the Goods left unsold had actually been all sold at
cost price. It should be debited to Valuation account,
and credited to Goods account. It is one of the Final
Assets.

But occasionally the Valuation is not given, but has
to be found from the **quantities** bought and sold. Then,
on *both sides* of the Goods account the values must be
set down at *cost* price, and the selling price entirely
ignored. The excess of the Debit or Buying Side over
the Credit or Selling Side (reckoning sales as well as
purchases at *cost* price) must be the value at cost price of
what is left unsold. In other words, to find the Valuation
of Stock from *quantities*, make out, on a detached slip
of paper, a new Goods account. Its Buying or Debit side
must be the same as that in the Ledger. But its Credit
or Selling Side must show what the Goods sold would
have realised if sold at *cost* price, wholly disregarding their
actual selling price. Then the excess of the Buying Side
over the Selling Side, since both are calculated at the
cost prices, must give the value at cost price of what
remains unsold. This Debit Balance is a Final Asset for
Final Balance Sheet. The fact of Goods account having
a Debit Balance which is an Asset, shows that it is one
of the *Single*-Entry Set of accounts. When, after crediting
to it value of stock on hand, this account is balanced and
closed in the Ledger, its *Credit* Excess, showing Gross
Profit on the sales, indicates an addition to Proprietor's
Capital. This fact shows that Goods account is also one

of the *Double*-Entry Set; it is a part of *the Proprietor's own personal account*, which shows on the Credit side (the side in favour of the person whose name heads the account) what the business owes him, either as Initial Capital, or as profit (*i.e. addition* to Initial Capital). Whenever, at close of books, the whole of Stock has been sold out, the Goods account is then a Double-Entry account, and nothing more. But in a Contract account (another Goods account), money spent on an *open* contract is treated as money spent on Goods left unsold (*i.e.* as an *Asset*); whereas part payment, or an advance received on account of an open contract, is a *Liability*, for the greater the amount received, the less to be received. As then Goods account may, and generally does, have a Balance for Final Balance Sheet, it belongs to the Single-Entry accounts as well as to the Double-Entry Set.

Comparative Unimportance of Transactions whose two Entries are confined to the Same Set of Accounts.

Every transaction that increases or lessens Final Net Capital must be debited in a *Single-Entry* account, and credited in a *Double-Entry* account, or *vice versâ*. And every transaction whose debit entry and credit entry both occur in the Double-Entry Set, or both in the Single-Entry Set, has no effect whatever in lessening or increasing what I am worth at close of books. For, suppose I debit either of the Single-Entry accounts with £20. My *Final Assets* are increased by that amount.

But my *Final Net Capital* is also increased by £20, and therefore one of the accounts relating to Capital must have £20 entered on the gain or credit side. Similarly, crediting either of the Single-Entry accounts increases Liabilities and lessens Capital, and one of the accounts relating to Capital must be debited. When I write off £80 depreciation on my shop, I credit Valuation account, one of the Single-Entry Set, and debit Profit and Loss account, one of the Double-Entry Set; this lessens Final Net Capital by £80, and both sets of accounts are equally affected. But when I buy a van for £20 I credit Cash account and debit Valuation account, both accounts belonging to the Single-Entry Set. Here no difference whatever is made in what I am worth, for I have £20 in my van just as before I had £20 in gold—the same property in another place and form. If I charge against profits interest on the money I lend to my business, and put it among my losses, as I should if the money were borrowed, and credit my own Personal or Capital account with the interest due but not paid, I debit Profit and Loss with the interest and credit Capital account with it, and both entries come in accounts belonging to the same set, the Double-Entry Set. Here, again, the entries cancel one another, so far as the Final Net Capital is concerned, for I enter the same amount as a loss, and once more as a gain. I lessen my profits and increase my Initial Capital by equal amounts in both cases. A full appreciation of the necessity of every gain or loss transaction appearing *in both sets of accounts* will save the learner from many errors. It is a truth of prime importance.

Why Called Fictitious.

If a draper, on reopening his Ledger, has Goods on hand worth £400, cash £600, Trade Plant and Fixtures worth £100, and Book Debts due to him £300, but himself owes £200, his Assets are £1400, his Liabilities £200, and his Initial Net Capital £1200. Each Asset is debited and each Liability credited (with the single exception of Goods on hand) to one or other of the Single-Entry accounts. The Goods must be debited to Trade account in the Double-Entry Set, because otherwise *profit* could not be ascertained. Each entry represents property; some I already have, some I am pretty certain to get, some I shall have to part with. But when I enter on the Cr. side of Capital account the resultant or combined effect of all these entries, when I write, By Sundries, Initial Net Capital £1200, I am entering *a second time over what does not exist in duplicate*, but once only. It is quite true that the draper has a commencing Capital of £1200, but not apart from, not in addition to, the Assets and Liabilities first entered. The Credit Entry in Capital account is fictitious only in being a re-entry of property once entered already. But it represents actual property nevertheless.

If I sell Goods for another man apart from my own Trade account, and am paid £20 commission, this is all clear gain or addition to commencing capital. I therefore enter £20 among my gains on the Cr. side of Profit and Loss; my Cashier having received the actual money, I debit his account £20. The record is double, but the transaction is one, and only £20 has come in.

Suppose my premises are mortgaged for £500 at 5 per cent. I have to pay the Mortgagee £25 every year for the use of his money. This is dead loss or lessening of Initial Capital, and £25 must be entered on the Dr. side of Profit and Loss account. Cashier has paid away £25, and credits his account £25. Profit and Loss account is debited £25, Cash account credited £25. One fact appears twice over.

When I pay my year's rent, £60, Cashier credits his account because he parts with money; but I also debit Profit and Loss Account £60—*i.e.*, enter £60 among my losses or lessenings of Initial Capital, because this payment makes me £60 worse off than I should be if my shop were my own and I had no rent to pay. It is money parted with without anything tangible coming back to me in return. In the Double-Entry account it is recorded *in the abstract* as lessening Capital; in the Single-Entry account we register *the concrete form*, the actual paying away of coins. The record is double.

If I draw out of my business £30 to live upon, Cashier pays it away to me, and credits his account £30; but I must enter it over again, and show its effect in lessening Initial Capital. I must not enter it with Trade losses, but debit my own Personal or Capital account £30. There is no fiction here, but a Double Entry.

If I take out of Stock £3 worth of Goods to cut up for trade patterns or samples, I credit Goods account £3, because £3 worth of Goods has been parted with as much as if sold. But I also debit Profit and Loss account £3, because I am £3 worse off by this transaction; my Initial Capital has been lessened by £3. Here both entries come in the Double-Entry Set of accounts, and the case seems an exception to the rule that every transaction involving addition to Capital, or the reverse, must be debited in one Set and credited in the other. It is, however, no exception, as will be shown later on in the article on Goods taken from Stock. The Double-Entry accounts, then, are fictitious only in being "doubles" of what appears elsewhere. They record in the *abstract* what is elsewhere recorded in the *concrete*. They register every transaction as increasing or lessening *Capital*. They answer the questions, What am I worth? Have I increased or lessened what I began with? Has this transaction made me better off or worse off? Whereas the Single-Entry accounts answer such questions as these:—If I am worth so much, *in what form* do I possess it? What are the actual properties? What cash have I? How much at Bank? How much in permanent Assets, such as buildings, horses and vans, fixtures, etc.? How much owing to me? Answers are given in Balance Account, a summary of the Single-Entry accounts.

Balance Account.   Equalising Entries. Transferring these Entries.

The Balance *Account* differs from Final Balance *Sheet* in having the Assets on the left-hand or Debit side, whereas Final Balance *Sheet* has Assets to the right. Many book-keepers do not open any Balance account, because the Final Balance Sheet shows the same facts only on opposite sides. But if we wish to show the double of *every* entry we make, even of the equalising entries we make when balancing, we open *a Balance account*. To the debit side of this we transfer every equalising entry made on the credit side of any of the Single-Entry accounts, and to its credit side every equalising entry made on the Debit side of any of them. If in Cash account there is a debit Excess of £200, showing that £200 more cash has been received than has been paid away, there will be an equalising entry on the credit side of £200 to make both sides equal. This Credit equalising entry finds its double in a Debit entry in Balance account. If in Grover's account there is a Credit Excess of £70, showing that I owe Grover £70, there will be a Debit equalising entry of £70 to make both sides equal ; and this will find its double in a Credit entry of £70 in Balance account. As, therefore, a *Credit* equalising entry proves a *Debit* balance, and is transferred to the debit side of Balance account, we express the law of transference in another way when we say that Debit Balances are taken to the debit side of Balance account, and Credit Balances to its credit side. And Balance account may be described as a mere summary or collection of Assets on the debit side, and Credits on the credit side, the excess of Assets over Liabilities at close showing Final Net Capital. But this Credit equalising entry in Balance account must have a double. It is found in the Debit equalising entry in Capital account, for both entries show Final Net Capital, but arrived at in different ways.

In the Double-Entry accounts, the Excesses are trans-

ferred from Trade account to Profit and Loss, and from
Profit and Loss to Capital account.   Gross Profit is added
to other profits, Net Profit to Capital.   Credit Excess from
Trade account goes to the credit side of Profit and Loss
account ; Credit Excess from Profit and Loss account goes
to the credit side of Capital account.   But in the language
of Bookkeeping, the Debit equalising entry in Trade
account finds its "double" in the Credit entry Gross
Profit in the Profit and Loss account ; and the Debit
equalising entry in Profit and Loss account finds its
"double" in the Credit entry Net Profit in Capital
account.   Finally, the Debit equalising entry in Capital
account finds its "double" in the Credit entry in
Balance account, Final Net Capital, Excess of Assets
over Liabilities.

Goods taken from Stock by Owner.   Goods taken for Trade Samples.   Goods returned not equal to Sample.   Goods Uninsured destroyed in Warehouse.   Goods Destroyed but Insured.

If I take £5 worth of Goods from Stock for my own
use, I have received £5 from my business, and must debit
my own personal account £5.   I must enter on the Dr.
side of Capital account, To Goods, £5.   This entry lessens
my Capital £5.   As Goods have been parted with, as if
sold to me and debited to me, I credit Goods account £5.
Both entries come in the Double-Entry Set.   So if I take
£5 worth of Goods for patterns, I must credit Goods
account £5.   But, as I use the patterns in my business,
I debit Profit and Loss account; I set £5 down among
T. P.

4

dead losses—money spent and nothing whatever coming back for it. Both entries are in the Double-Entry Set. If £5 worth of Goods is destroyed and uninsured, I debit Profit and Loss account £5 and credit Goods account £5, as if sold for nothing, given away, or stolen. Both entries, again, are in the Double-Entry Set. This seems contrary to the rule that every transaction increasing or lessening Capital must have one entry in one Set and the second entry in the other Set. But it is no exception. I have in all three cases lessened my Capital by £5. If the transaction is recorded in the Double-Entry Set only, how will the Final Assets and Liabilities in the Single-Entry Set show the lessened Capital, if no notice is taken of the transaction in them? It will record the transaction, *when stock is taken*, by a smaller Balance of Goods left unsold debited to Valuation account; that asset will be £5 less than it would otherwise be. Supposing we could rely on an accurate valuation, we need not credit them to Goods account at all, for a careful valuation would set matters right. Say the Goods left unsold would have been £200 worth but for these destroyed or taken away. £200 would then have been credited to Goods account and debited to Valuation account as an Asset. Whereas now £195 are credited to Goods and debited to Valuation. There is £5 less in the Asset, and there is £5 less profit in Goods account. The Goods account, if not credited with £5 when the Goods were destroyed, will have £5 less on its Cr. or selling side, and this means £5 less profit on balancing. If £5 less is taken as profit from Goods account, the effect will be just the same on Capital as crediting the Goods when destroyed so as to have £5 more profit from Goods, and debiting Profit and Loss £5; for the Debit neutralises the Credit. Hence this is certainly no exception.

When I return to Bryan £12 worth of Goods I have bought of him, because not equal to sample, I debit the receiver Bryan and credit Goods. The Goods are re-sold to Bryan at cost price. When Goods insured for £500, but valued at £600, are destroyed, I credit Goods as if sold to the insurers for £500, and debit Cash £500; or debit Cash £500, debit Profit and Loss £100, and credit Goods £600. The effect on Capital is the same in both cases. When permanent Assets are destroyed, their whole value must be written off or credited to Valuation account, because the whole Asset set forth in the Debit must be cancelled. If my warehouse, valued at £1000 but insured for £400 only, is burnt down, I credit Valuation account £1000, because the whole £1000 Debit must be cancelled; I debit Cash account £400, and Profit and Loss is debited £600. In the Single-Entry Set an Asset of £1000 disappears for one of £400; in the Double-Entry Set a loss of £600 is put with the other losses to diminish Capital by that amount. The same fact is represented first as lessening an Asset, then over again as lessening Capital.

Interest charged on Capital.

If I invest £2000 in my business, I am entitled to debit to Profit and Loss account, as a first charge upon profits, reasonable interest on what I lend. If I borrowed the money and paid 3 per cent., I should pay £60 a year to the lender, and as this would be a dead loss to me, I should credit Cash £60 and debit Profit and Loss £60. And if my clear profits came to £60 only, I should say I made no profit at all by trading, for I could get £60 interest by putting my money in a Bank and taking my ease. On closing books, then, I debit Profit and Loss £60, and credit Capital account £60, just as I should credit the account of the lender if I did not promptly pay him. If I take the £60 interest out of my business, I simply credit Cash account and debit Profit and Loss £60 each. If I leave it in the business, it is really additional Capital. Now, the whole of the Double-Entry Set may be grouped together as one single account, so far as final result is concerned. Hence, debiting one side £60 and crediting the other side £60 does not affect Final Net Capital at all. It is counting £60 as a loss, and then adding £60 as gain or addition to Capital. I am neither better nor worse off; my Final Capital is the same, but *my profits seem £60 less*. If any change were made in Final Capital, one of the Single-Entry Set must have received an entry, for the excess of Assets over Liabilities would have been disturbed.

Trade Expenses: Salaries, Wages, Advertisements, Rent, Repairs, Rates, Taxes, Insurance, Carriage, Paper, Twine, Stamps, Stationery, etc.

All money spent on these is debited to Profit and Loss as *a dead loss*, money going out without anything saleable coming back in return. It is credited to Cash account, if paid. If due, but not paid, it must be credited to the person to whom it is owing, to the creditor. *But it must never be debited to the person who receives the payment, unless he has first been credited with it.* Unless told otherwise, we always assume that such payments are ready-money payments, and ready-money payments are seldom booked as *personal accounts*, because the account opens and closes simultaneously as regards the person. The only accounts concerned are Cash which is paid away, and *my own Personal account*, or a part of it, the Profit and Loss account, which is debited, because *my Capital is lessened* by the Payment of these Trade Expenses. If I pay £70 for trade utensils which will last many years, I get back something saleable for my money; I debit Valuation account, and credit Cash account each with £70; *the person I bought it of has no account in my books.* Here I have only changed an asset in gold into an asset in utensils, and I am neither worse off nor better off. But when I pay the newspaper proprietor for advertising, or the insurance office for insuring, or my clerk for his services, nothing saleable comes back, and I debit Profit and Loss account, and credit Cash account with the amount paid away. The debit entry in Profit and Loss means that the transaction has made me so much worse off. When I pay £70 rent promptly, the Landlord has that very day become my creditor for £70, and when I pay him £70 he becomes my debtor for £70, and the account is closed and done with. If I debited an account opened for the Landlord, without having first credited it, the debit would be an asset of mine; it would mean that the Landlord owed me £70! No personal account must be debited unless that debit, if it stood alone, would mean so much money owing to the owner of the books; *i.e.,* unless it is an asset of his.

When one of several partners receives a fixed salary as a prior charge on profits, say £100, if he does not draw it out, it must be credited to his own Personal or Capital account, and debited to Profit and Loss. If he draws it out, it must be debited to Profit and Loss, and credited to Cash account. It does not then come into the Partner's Capital account, for it is a ready-money transaction. To debit it to his Capital account would be absurd, for that would mean that he has drawn out of his Capital £100, whereas he has only been paid a salary as a clerk is paid, and his Capital and share of profits have not been lessened by £100, but by his own share of that charge. If he is not actually paid, the effect of debiting Profit and Loss £100 and crediting his account £100 is to increase his Capital £100, *minus* his own share of the expense incurred by the firm in paying him.

Bad Debts; Bankruptcies; Dishonoured Bills and Cheques; Debts Recovered Unexpectedly.

If Grover, owing me £30, absconds, and I feel sure I shall never get any of the money, I must not keep on my books a worthless asset. I credit Grover's account *as if paid*, but instead of writing By Cash £30, I write By Profit and Loss £30, meaning that I have added it to my losses, as a lessening of Capital in the Double-Entry accounts. In the Single-Entry Set an Asset of £30 is removed. If Digby, owing me £60, compounds with his creditors and pays 15s. in the £, I close Digby's account, crediting it with the whole £60 *to cancel the entire Asset on the Debit side*, because I shall never get any more than I now get, and must not let any balance remain as due. Cash is debited £45, Profit and Loss is debited £15, because a dead loss of £15 is incurred. If Roper buys Goods of me, and pays me by cheque £20, and on presenting the cheque the Banker declines to cash it, I open an account for Roper, and debit him £20; he owes me £20, because I gave him £20 worth of Goods for a worthless piece of paper. I must not reckon it as a loss until I find Roper cannot pay me. If I hold an Acceptance of Davis's, a Bill stamped and signed by him promising to pay me £250 at a stated time and place, and he dishonours his Bill by failing to pay me when I present the Bill, I do not treat this as a loss at present. I debit Davis as owing me £250 *plus* any expenses he puts me to. I credit the Bills Receivable account, not because I give back the Bill to the Acceptor, as I should do if honoured, but because the Asset contained in the Debit entry in that account *must be cancelled*. It no longer exists as a Bill. It has been transferred to Davis's Personal account, and must not be in both.

If, after marking off Grover's account as a bad debt, Grover pays me the £30, I debit Cash account, and credit either Profit and Loss or Capital account. Some object to credit Profit and Loss, because it is not an ordinary

trade profit, and prefer to consider it as increase to Capital.
The effect is the same either way: I have the money, and
my Capital is increased.

Discount, Interest, Commission.

When Bryant owes me £45, and pays me £42, I, allowing
him £3 discount for early payment, lose £3, because I
get £3 less than I have booked as belonging to me.
I debit Profit and Loss £3, debit Cash £42, and credit
Bryant's account with the whole £45 to cancel Bryant's
whole debt. On the other hand, if I owe Ballard £100,
and he accepts £95 *as a complete settlement*, I gain £5,
for I have booked Ballard as my creditor for the whole
£100. I debit Ballard with the whole £100 to cancel
the whole liability, and credit Cash £95 and Profit and
Loss £5. If I charge £1 interest on an overdue debt
of £20, and receive £21 from Lloyd, I close Lloyd's
account by crediting it with £20, I credit Profit and Loss
£1, and debit Cashier with £21. Here is an increase to
Capital in the Double-Entry Set, and an increased asset in
the Single-Entry Set. On the other hand, when I pay
£30 interest on mortgage, that is dead loss; £30 debited
to Profit and Loss, £30 credited to Cash. When I sell
Goods for another on Commission, that is clear gain to
be credited to Profit and Loss. I must not credit the
Consignor's account unless I have first debited him as
owing me the Commission. If I credit his account it
will mean that I owe him that amount.

When my Banker allows me interest on my deposit,
that is clear gain to be credited to Profit and Loss

account, and debited to Bank, like an additional deposit. On the contrary, if Banker allows me to overdraw my account and charges me £5 interest on the money he lends me, that is a dead loss to be debited to Profit and Loss and credited to Bank account. I owe Banker £5; I have diminished my capital by £5, and have £5 to deduct from any amount I may hereafter send to the Bank.

Depreciation; Damage; Death of Live Stock; Shipwreck or Foundering.

Among my Assets is a Lease for twenty-one years, valued at £800. This will get less valuable every year, and 5 per cent. depreciation must be written off its value; £40 is debited to Profit and Loss, £40 credited to Valuation account to lessen the Asset £800 on the Dr. side. A horse debited to Valuation account as worth £70 gets killed. Valuation account must be credited £70 to lessen the Asset, Profit and Loss must be debited £70 to lessen Capital. A ship debited to Valuation account as worth £5000, but insured for £3000 only, founders at sea. £3000 is due from Underwriters, £2000 is dead loss. Debit Underwriters £3000, debit Profit and Loss £2000; credit Valuation £5000 to cancel the whole Asset. If a flock of sheep is debited in Valuation account as worth £2000, and a murrain destroys £600 worth of them, £600 must be credited to Valuation account to lessen the Asset, and debited to Profit and Loss to lessen Capital by £600. Whenever an asset disappears without reappearing in another account, the loss must be entered on the Debit side of one of the Double-Entry Set.

Must I debit Profit and Loss or Trade Account?
—Wages in a Manufacturer's books are debited to Trade
account; so the dairymaid's wages in a Dairy account.
Duty paid on spirits, cartage of goods, etc., increase the
buying price, and are debited to Goods account. Travel-
ling expenses incurred in buying are debited sometimes
to Trade account, sometimes to Profit and Loss account.
Consequently the pupil must not expect his GROSS PROFIT
to agree with that given in solutions, in all cases. But the
net Profit must agree.

A VERY SIMPLE LEDGER POSTED, AND PROVED CORRECT BY TRIAL BALANCE.

[*Adapted from Question B, Society of Arts Examination Paper,* 1892.]

After the method of Double Entry, find the Gross Profit, the Net
Profit, and Final Net Capital of the fruit dealer whose transactions are
recorded below, supposing on Tuesday night he had 10*s.* 4*d.* cash,
besides some apples on hand worth 8*d.*

His Initial Capital is 11*s.* Credit Capital account 11*s.*; debit
Cash account 10*s.* 4*d.*; debit Goods account 8*d.*

On Wednesday morning he purchased additional stock to the value
of 9*s.* 4*d.*

Debit Goods account 9*s.* 4*d.*; credit Cash account 9*s.* 4*d.*

He paid an attendant in the market 2*d.* for watching his barrow, and
expended 4*d.* on oil and wick for his lamp.

Trade Expenses. Debit P. &. L. 6*d.*; credit Cash account 6*d.*

He bought paper bags to the amount of 6*d.*, one-third of which he
used in the course of the day.

Trade Expenses. Debit P. & L. 6*d.*; credit Cash 6*d.* Then
credit P. & L. 4*d.* for bags remaining; debit Valuation account
4*d.* as a remaining asset. (See Appendix Note 1, p. 126.)

His sales amounted to 15*s.* 8*d.*

Debit Cash 15*s.* 8*d.* ; credit Goods 15*s.* 8*d.*

Out of which he paid 1*s.* 2*d.* for the rent of his barrow,

Trade Expense. Debit P. & L. 1*s.* 2*d.* ; credit Cash 1*s.* 2*d.*,

and had apples left unsold of the cost value of 1*s.* 4*d.*

Credit Goods account 1*s.* 4*d.* as if sold ; debit Valuation account 1*s.* 4*d.* as a remaining asset.

D͞r̠   CAPITAL ACCOUNT.   C͞r̠

Against him.	*In Owner's favour.*		
		s.	d.
	By Sundries	11	0

PROFIT AND LOSS ACCOUNT.

Losses.				*Gains.*		
		s.	d.		s.	d.
To Cash (minder)...	...	0	2	By Valuation (bags left) ...	0	4
„ „ (oil) ...	...	0	4			
„ „ (bags) ...	...	0	6			
„ „ (rent) ...	...	1	2			

GOODS OR TRADE ACCOUNT.

Buying Side.				*Selling Side.*		
		s.	d.		s.	d.
To Capital...	...	0	8	By Cash	15	8
„ Cash ...	...	9	4	„ Valuation (on hand) ...	1	4

VALUATION ACCOUNT.

Receiving Side.			*Paying-away Side.*
	s.	d.	
To Goods on hand ...	1	4	
„ P. and L. (bags left)...	0	4	

CASH ACCOUNT.

Receiving Side.			s.	d.	Paying-away Side.			s.	d.
To Capital...	...	...	10	4	By Goods ...	...	...	9	4
„ Goods ...	...	...	15	8	„ P. & L....	...	...	0	2
					„ „ ...	...	...	ɔ	4
					„ „ ...	...	...	0	6
					„ „ ...	...	...	1	2

Dr TRIAL BALANCE. Cr

£	s.	d.		s.	d.	
—	—	—	Capital Account	11	0	Excess of Credits, 16s. 2d.
0	2	2	Profit and Loss Account ...	0	4	
0	10	0	Goods Account	17	0	
Excess of Debits, 16s. 2d.	0	1	8	Valuation Account ...	—	
	1	6	0	Cash Account	11	6
Grand Total Debits, £1	19	10		£1	19	10 Grand Total Credits.

Books prove correct, because

(1) Grand Total Debits equal Grand Total Credits.

(2) Excess of Credits over Debits in the Double-Entry Set
equals the Excess of Debits over Credits in the
Single-Entry Set — i.e., Capital plus Profits—minus
Losses equals Assets minus Liabilities.

Gross Profit = Credit Excess of Goods Account.

= 17s. minus 10s. = 7s.

Net Profit = Credit Excess of P. & L. Account.

= 7s. + 4d. — 2s. 2d. = 5s. 2d.

Final Net Capital = 16s. 2d.

FINAL BALANCE SHEET.

Liabilities.		s.	d.	Assets.			s.	d.
Balance, Final Net Capital		16	2	Valuation	...	...	1	8
				Cash	...	...	14	6
							16	2

D^r	BALANCE ACCOUNT.			C^r	
		s.	d.		s. d.
To Valuation ...	...	1	8	By Final Net Capital	16 2
,, Cash	...	14	6		
		16	2		

THE JOURNAL AND JOURNALISING.

THE Ledger, being more pictorial than the Journal, conveys to the eye more readily the state of one's affairs, and should first be mastered. But in Government offices, and many counting-houses, nothing is posted into the Ledger until i has "passed through the Journal." In the Journal every transaction is entered, first as a Debit, then as a Credit, either in order of time, or as taken from Cash Book, Bank Book, Sales Book, Purchases Book, etc., at the end of the week or the month. As the Journal contains exactly the same Debits and the same Credits as the Ledger, only differently arranged, the Totals of the Journal must agree with the Ledger Totals in Trial Balance, and error is certain in either of the following cases :—

(1) If the *Journal* Debits do not equal the *Journal* Credits as grand totals.

(2) If the *Ledger* Debits in Trial Balance do not equal the *Ledger* Credits.

(3) If all *four totals* are not exactly alike.

(4) If the Excess of *Credits* over Debits in the Double-Entry Set does not equal the Excess of *Debits* over Credits in the Single-Entry Set.

These are the four methods of proving books. The Journal can best be studied in the Practical Part.

Passing the Closing Entries, or Equalising Entries, through the Journal.

Beginning with Goods account, a *Debit* equalising entry of 7s. is required to make both sides equal. This means that there is a *Credit* Excess or Gross Profit of 7s. in Goods account to be carried into Profit and Loss account, and placed with other profits on its Cr. side. The equalising entry, 7s., on the Dr. side of Goods has its "double" in the 7s. entered as Gross Profit on the Cr. side of Profit and Loss account. In Profit and Loss account, after the 7s. have been taken to its Cr. side, a Debit equalising entry of 5s. 2d. is required to make both sides equal. This shows a Credit Excess, an Excess of Profits over Losses, a Net Profit of 5s. 2d. to be carried to the Cr. side of Capital to increase it. The Debit equalising entry of 5s. 2d. in Profit and Loss account has its "double" in the Credit entry of 5s. 2d. in Capital account. In this account, after taking 5s. 2d. to its Cr. side, a Debit equalising entry of 16s. 2d. is required to make both sides equal. This means that Final Net Capital is 16s. 2d., as seen also in Balance account, where Assets and Liabilities are collected together. The excess of Assets over Liabilities is also 16s. 2d.; and the Debit entry of 16s. 2d. in Capital account has its "double" in the Credit equalising entry of 16s. 2d. required in Balance account to make the Asset side and Liability side equal.

In the Single-Entry accounts, Valuation account requires a *Credit* equalising entry of 1s. 8d.; this finds its "double" in the *Debit* entry of 1s. 8d. in Balance account. In Cash account a Credit equalising entry of 14s. 6d. is required; this, too, finds its "double" in the Debit entry of 14s. 6d. in Balance account. In Balance account, as there are no Liabilities in this case, the Credit equalising entry is 16s. 2d., and this we have already seen finds its "double" in the Debit equalising entry of 16s. 2d. in Capital account. In both cases the amount is 16s. 2d., but it has been arrived at in very different ways. In one way we obtained it from what we had at first, and what we have added to it since; in the other, by showing the actual property or assets.

JOURNAL ENTRIES FOR BALANCING AND CLOSING.

Dr.				Cr.		
£	s.	d.		£	s.	d.
0	16	2	Balance account Dr.			
			To Valuation Cr.	0	1	8
			,, Cash Cr.	0	14	6
0	16	2	Capital account Dr.			
			To Balance account Cr.	0	16	2
0	5	2	Profit and Loss Dr.			
			To Capital account Cr.	0	5	2
0	7	0	Goods account Dr.			
			To Profit and Loss Cr.	0	7	0
Total Debits	£2 4 6			Total Credits	£2 4 6	

Caution !—The learner must not allow himself to be misled by the peculiar phrases of Bookkeeping. If, on closing books, I owe Roberts £12, there is a Credit balance in Roberts' account in my books, and a *Debit* equalising entry of £12 to be transferred to the Cr. side of Balance account among Liabilities. This would be journalised :—

> £12 Roberts, Dr.
>> To Balance account Cr. £12.

The expression " Roberts, Dr." does not mean that Roberts is my debtor, for he is my creditor : I owe him £12. It means that in Roberts's account there is a *Debit equalising entry* of £12 to be transferred to the Cr. side of Balance account as one of my Liabilities.

If in Draper's account there is a Debit balance of £50, Draper owes me £50, and there will be a Credit equalising entry of £50 to be transferred to the Debit side of Balance account as one of my Assets. This would be journalised :—

> £50 Balance account Dr.
>> To Draper, Cr. £50.

The expression " Draper, Cr." does not mean that Draper is my creditor, for he is actually my debtor : he owes me £50. It is Double-Entry language. The "Cr." refers to the equalising entry in Draper's account, and a Credit equalising entry shows a Debit balance, and a Debit balance in a Single-Entry account shows a debt due to me, or an asset of mine. Any of the Closed Ledgers in the Practical Part will illustrate this.

Combinations in Posting and Journalising.

When several transactions occur the same day belonging to different persons, or affecting different accounts, but all

falling on the same side of the Ledger, and all having their
"double" in one and the same account on the opposite
side, those falling in different accounts may have their
"double" in one inclusive total on the opposite side.
Thus :—

> June 20. (*d*) Bought of Smith, Goods, £15.
> Sold Gibson, Goods, £25 (*c*).
> Sold Prior, Goods, £10 (*c*).
> (*d*) Bought for Cash, Goods, £5.
> (*d*) Bought of Rylands, Goods, £30.
> Sold for Cash, Goods, £12 (*c*).

Transactions marked (*d*) can all be debited collectively
those marked (*c*) credited collectively.

*D*ʳ   June 20.

£50   Goods, Dr.   *C*ʳ

> To Smith,   Cr., £15.
> ,, Cash,   Cr.,   5.
> ,, Rylands, Cr.,   30.

25   Gibson, Dr.
10   Prior,   Dr.
12   Cash,   Dr.

> ,, Goods,   Cr.,   47.

When the Journal is not written up day by day, but
compiled at the week's end or month's end from the Cash
Book, Sales Book, Purchases Book, etc., the number of
the entries can be much lessened, and much time saved,
by grouping together in this way. A pattern Journal with
transactions grouped together, when similar, is given in the
Practical Part.

T. P.

On making the Two Entries TALLY in Posting, to facilitate finding a Debit from its " Double " on the Credit Side, and vice versa.

Every entry must be so worded as to show in what account that same transaction will be found recorded on the opposite side of the Ledger. If in crediting Cash account £20 I write By Landlord £20, I ought on finding Landlord's account to see £20 debited to him. If I find no such account, I conclude that the rent was promptly paid, the transaction was a ready-money one, and not booked at all as concerning the Landlord, but debited to Profit and Loss as lessening my Capital by £20 : money out, nothing back in its place. The proper Credit entry would be By Profit and Loss £20. The wrong entry suggests what is false, that the rent was not promptly paid, and that I opened an account for the Landlord, and credited it £20.

Similarly, every entry on the Cr. side must show in what account I shall find the corresponding Dr. entry. If a horse worth £60, and debited as such in Valuation account, is no longer one of my Assets, the entry I make on the Credit side of Valuation to lessen my Assets down on the Debit side, depends upon where the corresponding debit entry is made, and must say in which account. If the horse has been killed I write " By Profit and Loss "; if sold for cash I write " By Cash."

So also every debit entry must state in what account the corresponding *credit* entry occurs. When £30 cash is debited, the entry must be "To Goods" if Goods account is credited £30 for a sale; it must be "To Thompson" if Thompson is credited as having paid it to me; it must be "To Profit and Loss' if paid me as commission, and so a clear addition to Capital; it must be "To Capital account" if it appears on the credit side of Capital account as a sum added to original capital, not from the business; it must be "To Valuation account" if I have sold any of my fixtures, utensils, vans, horses, etc.; it must be "To Bank" if withdrawn from Bank account; "To Bills Receivable" if received when one of my debtors honours his acceptance.

If the pupil doubts what entry to make when debiting, let him ask "In what account will it be credited?" when crediting, "In what account will it be debited?"

The only exception made to this rule is when several postings are combined: we then write "By Sundries" or "To Sundries." We mean that the corresponding entry will not be found in one account, but several. This, though vague, is not misleading, or suggestive of what is untrue.

On the Interpretation of Entries, or Translating Bookkeeping Language into Ordinary Speech.

It is useful when posting straight from Waste Book to say what would be the *Journal entry* before posting any item or transaction. So also the learner should often open a Ledger at random, and fixing now upon a debit, now on a credit, relate in ordinary language what transaction it records, and how it affects each of the two accounts

concerned.   He should open a Journal and do likewise.
If he finds—

£50 Capital Dr.   To Cash Cr. £50.

he might say, £50 Cash has been paid away, for Cash
account is credited.   It has lessened owner's Capital, for
it is debited to Capital; put on the same side as *net losses.*
Owner has received £50; taken it out of his business,
and has £50 less in the business.   If the cash had been
paid to a creditor, that creditor's account would be
debited; if for goods, Goods account would be debited;
if for a horse, Valuation account; if for trade expenses,
Profit and Loss; if paid to the owner, the owner's account,
Capital account, is debited.

If he finds posted on the Cr. side of Timms's account,
" By Profit and Loss, £25," he might reason thus:—
Timms seems credited with having paid away £25.   But
to whom?   Not to Cashier, or his account would be
debited; not to Banker, or Banker's account would be
debited.   The Debit Entry in Profit and Loss shows that
I have *lost* £25 by Timms.   He has paid nothing.   His
bad debt is written off as worthless, and my Capital is
lessened by £25.

On the Dr. side of Bills Receivable account, he finds
posted "To Goods £120," and might reason thus:—A
Bill for £120 has been received as paper money in pay·
ment for goods the acceptor of the bill has bought.   This
bill, *for the present,* settles the account.   On the Credit
or Selling side of Goods account, I find £120 opposite
the entry " By Bill Receivable."   This Bill owner may

endorse and sell, pay it away for its present value, or keep till mature, and then, receiving the money for it, give it back to the acceptor. Meanwhile it is one of his assets.

On the Debit side of Bills Payable account, he finds the entry "To Prior £500," and might reason like this. Owner has received back an Acceptance of his own, promising to pay £500 to one of his creditors. He would not get it back if he had not paid, or virtually paid. He gets it from Prior. Turning to Prior's account, on the Credit side is the entry "By Bill Payable £500." I see Prior is deep in the owner's debt, and pays £500 of it by returning owner's own Acceptance for £500, then in Prior's hands. Owner now cancels the Liability entered on Credit side of Bills Payable account when he gave the Bill; he will not have to pay this now. On the other hand, Prior now owes him £500 less than before.

ERRORS WHICH THE DOUBLE-ENTRY TEST DOES NOT SHOW UP.

1. IF Brown pays me £5, and I credit Green £5 instead of crediting Brown, no difference will be made in Ledger totals or Journal totals, and the error may escape detection till Brown complains of being asked to pay too great a balance.

2. If Cashier receives £10 from French, and neither debits his own account with it, nor credits French's, but pockets the money, this may not be discovered until

French complains. If honestly put in cash-box, the error will be discovered when cash is counted at night. There will be £10 more in box than down in books.

3. If I mistake a sale for a purchase, or *vice versa*, and book correctly on the false assumption, both sides of Ledger and Journal are *equally* wrong, and agree. If when Goods worth £20 are *sold* to Evans on credit, I enter them as if *bought* of Evans on credit, I represent myself £40 worse off than I am, both in the Double-Entry Set of accounts and the Single-Entry Set. My Purchase Book and Sales Book will set me right, and Evans, if honest, will point it out.

BILLS, ACCEPTANCES, DRAFTS, FOREIGN BILLS OF EXCHANGE, PAPER MONEY.

In Bookkeeping, *a Bill* is not an *Invoice*, such as a grocer sends out with Goods when delivered. It is *paper money* as much as a Bank Note or a Bank Cheque. It is a *negotiable instrument* which can be bought and sold, paid away for Goods bought, or received for Goods sold, just as a Bank Note passes from one person to another. Bills are of two kinds: (1) Promissory Notes; (2) Drafts or Acceptances. Specimens of each are given in the Practical Part. A Promissory Note is a stamped written *promise* to pay a stated sum at a stated time and place, *for value received*, to the creditor named on it, or *to his order*. It must be signed by the debtor, and is useless for transference unless it contains the words "or to his order," and of use to no one unless it contains the words "for value received." An *Acceptance* or Draft is a stamped written *order* addressed to the debtor by the creditor, bidding him pay to the creditor, or *to his order*, a stated sum at a stated time, *for value received*. It must contain the words "for value received," and "or to bearer," or "or to my order," and must carry a stamp, varying in cost with the amount of the Bill. It must also be signed by both debtor and creditor. The creditor writes his name at the foot of the order; the debtor writes his across the face of the order, and adds the words "Accepted, payable at such and such a Bank, or such and such a House." The creditor is said *to draw on the debtor* for the sum named on the Bill; the debtor *accepts* the obligation to pay it, and owns the debt. The debtor is the *Acceptor*, the drawee, or person drawn upon; he will have to pay the cash. The creditor is the *drawer*; the money will be paid to him, unless he parts with the Bill to another person. Then he *endorses* the Acceptance by writing his name *across the back* of it; and Acceptor will have to pay the cash to whoever may hold the Bill at the time of its falling due. If the Acceptor pays promptly, he *honours* his Acceptance; if he fails to pay, he *dishonours* it. Should he pay before he is in honour bound to pay, he *takes up*, or *retires* his Bill, and may have a little less to pay, as discount may be allowed him. If, when the time for payment draws near, he cannot pay all, but pays a part of the cash, and can induce the holder of the Bill to write out a new Bill giving him more time to pay the remainder, he *renews* his Acceptance. The Bill following

is Thomas King's Acceptance for £300 at three months.
It is drawn by Samuel Marks, the Creditor, on Thomas
King, the Debtor. On Jan. 7th, 1897 (unless that day
happens to be a Sunday, then on Jan. 6th), Thomas King
will have to pay £300, though not necessarily to Marks,
but to the holder of the Bill at that time. When King
has *accepted* the Bill by writing his name across the face
of it with the words "Accepted, payable at such and such
a Bank," he gives the Bill to Marks, who may either keep
it till Jan. 7th, sell it meanwhile for its then value, or pay
it away instead of cash. But if he parts with the Bill,
he must write "Samuel Marks" across *the back* of it, as
a pledge to the Endorsee, or buyer of the Bill, that the
Endorser will see the money is paid if the Acceptor
should fail.

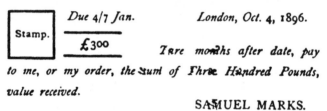

Sometimes a Bill is drawn by the Creditor in favour
of a third party, a Creditor of the Drawer. The following
is William Smith's acceptance of Henry Bryant's Draft,
favour of James Finch, for £80, which Smith will have
to pay to Finch or Finch's order, on Dec. 13th, 1896.

Due Dec. 10/13.   *London, Oct.* 10, 1896.

Stamp

£80

Two mouth after date, pay to James Finch, or his order, the sum of Eighty Pounds, value received.

HENRY BRYANT.

Mr. WILLIAM SMITH,
5, MOUNT STREET, HAMPSTEAD, N.W.

Smith hands this Bill to Finch, after signing it. If Finch gets his Banker to *discount* this Bill for £78, he *endorses* the Bill, and gives it to the Banker. Should Smith fail to pay the Banker on Dec. 13th, Finch will have to pay the Banker the whole £80, or, what is the same thing, credit the Banker's account £80 and debit Smith's account £80 in his books. Why does Finch refund more than £78 to the Banker? Because he received from the Banker £78 *plus* the use of £78 for two months; and the Banker would not have paid down £78 unless he had felt pretty sure of getting £80 in two months' time. Not only the Drawer of the Bill, but *every Endorser* becomes responsible for the payment of the money promised, and for all expenses incurred, if dishonoured by the Acceptor. The holder of the Acceptance, at the time it falls due, has to present it for payment at the place named on it, or his Banker presents it for him. When the holder's Banker returns a Bill dishonoured at Acceptor's Bank, a lawyer *Notes and Protests* the Bill for the holder. He makes a copy of the Bill, and on it a written statement that the Bill has been duly presented for payment, and payment refused; and that all parties to the Bill, Drawer, Acceptor, and each of the Endorsers, are liable to the holder for the amount promised *plus* costs. He also notes on the back of the dishonoured Bill the fact that it has been protested. This must be done in presence of two witnesses. *Three days of grace* are usually allowed. A Bill mature on March 1st is not legally due till March 4th, or March 3rd if a Saturday. Notice of dishonour must be immediately given to Drawer and every Endorser. But *protesting* is not absolutely necessary unless it is a dishonoured *foreign Bill of Exchange.*

The following is a foreign Bill of Exchange drawn by John Adams of London on William Ryder of New York, for £2000, favour of Thomas Friar, of New York, at one month. Ryder will have to pay on Jan. 4th, 1897, £2000 to Friar, or to whoever holds the Bill at that date But he makes the payment for Adams, his Creditor

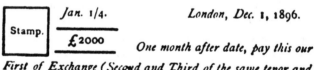

Stamp.	*Jan.* 1/4.		*London, Dec.* 1, 1896.
	£2000		

One month after date, pay this our First of Exchange (Second and Third of the same tenor and date not paid) to Mr. Thomas Friar, or his order, Two Thousand Pounds, value received, and debit the same to our account.

JOHN ADAMS.

Mr. WILLIAM RYDER,
    BROADWAY, NEW YORK.

Foreign Bills are usually drawn in triplicate, to provide against loss in transmission. Two copies are sent out by two successive packets; the third retained by the sender till the safe arrival or the loss of one of the others is announced. Paying by Bill is much easier and safer than sending gold across the seas. Suppose A, of London, trades with B and with C, both of Calcutta; and that B owes A £500 for goods A has sent him from London, and A owes C £500 for goods C has sent him from Calcutta. B is A's debtor, C is A's creditor, for the same amount. A draws upon B for £500, in favour of C, and sends the Draft to B. B accepts the Bill, and gives it to C. C can either sell this Bill and get paid at once, or wait till it is mature. This is a very simple instance, but similar transactions are going on constantly all the world over. A London timber merchant, T, owes £1000 to a merchant in St. Petersburg, P. T buys of a banker a Bill for £1000, on St. Petersburg—*i.e.* an Acceptance which will be honoured in St. Petersburg; the cash promised on it will be paid at a St. Petersburg bank.' He sends this to P. P takes it to the Bank and gets his money as soon as the term of the Bill expires; or he may get its present value at once. J, in Jamaica, owes L, in London, £941 18s. 5d. for a consignment of goods L has sent him. When L shipped the goods, he sent with them a draft on J for their supposed value, say £900. When J has sold them, he accepts L's draft for £900, credits L with the remaining £41 18s. 5d., which he still owes him, and sends him his Acceptance. When L gets J's Acceptance, a London banker will buy it of him, and thus he will get paid without any gold changing hands. Why will a London banker buy this piece of paper signed by J,

and what will he do with it? There are merchants in
London who have creditors in Jamaica, to whom they
would like to pay what they owe them without sending
over gold. They buy Bills on Jamaica, *i.e.* drawn on
persons in Jamaica, who will honour their Bills at a
Jamaica bank. These they send over to Jamaica to their
creditors. The creditor who receives J's Acceptance will
be paid £900 at J's bank, unless he gets paid earlier by
asking a banker to discount the Bill for him. A London
silk mercer, owing £300 to a Lyons manufacturer, buys
Bills on Lyons amounting to £300; a Manchester cotton
master, owing £800 to a New Orleans creditor, buys Bills
on New Orleans amounting to £800; a Melbourne iron-
monger, owing £500 to a Birmingham firm, buys, in
Melbourne, Bills worth £500 drawn on Birmingham or
London. If a Bristol trader had a banking account at
Chicago, and owed a Chicago merchant £400, he would
send to the latter a cheque for £400 on that bank.
That draft or cheque would be a Foreign Bill of Exchange, a Bill on Chicago. But it would be *a Short
Bill*, payable at sight, payable on demand, unless otherwise worded.

But in Bookkeeping a cheque goes into Bank account;
Promissory Notes and Acceptances into Bills account. A
cheque is assumed to be paid into Bank *the very day
it is received*. It is not treated as a negotiable instrument,
capable of being endorsed, and paid away again instead
of cash, as a Bill is. " I paid by cheque" means " I paid
by a draft on my own Banker." " I was paid by cheque"
refers to a "crossed, non-negotiable cheque," debited at

once to Bank account. " I paid by cheque " supposes the cheque *at once presented for payment*, and my Bank account credited (Banker's account in my books credited ; my account in Banker's books debited).

BILLS RECEIVABLE.

A BILL Receivable in my books represents money *I am to receive;* it is an *Asset* of mine, property not yet in possession, but about to be. As an Asset it appears on the *Debit or receiving side* of an account of its own, one of the Single-Entry Set. If Brown buys £200 worth of Goods of me, and pays with a Bill at three months instead of cash, I credit Goods account £200, and debit Bills Receivable account £200, because *I receive a Bill* worth that. *For the next three months I must consider the Goods paid for*, and the Asset £200 on the Debit side of Bills Receivable account as equal to £200 on the Debit side of Cash account. Why so? Because, if Brown's commercial name is good, I can, whenever I like, sell Brown's Acceptance, and get the cash, with a small reduction for Discount. If I sell it for £195, I lose £5. I debit Cash £195, debit Profit and Loss £5, and credit Bills Receivable £200. I credit Bills Receivable because *I part with the Bill*, and because I must cancel the Asset on the Debit side. The Asset now exists as Cash £195 ; the rest is gone. If I keep the Bill till mature, I get £200 for Cashier or Banker, and give back Brown his Acceptance. Cash or Bank is then debited £200, and Bills

Receivable account credited £200. But if Brown dishonours my draft on him, I then open a *Personal account* for Brown and debit him £200, for he owes me the promised money. I must also credit Bills Receivable account, though I *do not* part with the Bill. Why? To neutralise or cancel the Asset on the Debit side. That Asset no longer exists as a Bill. It goes from this account, and appears as a personal debt. Of course it must not appear in both accounts. My Credit entry in Bills Receivable account is "By Brown £200."

If, during the three months, I got £250 into Brown's debt, and had Brown's Acceptance still in my possession, I could partly pay Brown by returning it to him cancelled. Brown would then not have anything to pay me, and I should virtually be paying him £200 towards what I owe him. I should then, as before, debit Brown £200, and credit Bills Receivable £200. A Bill Receivable has gone out from the business.

But why do we not regard a Bill Receivable as the *personal debt* of the Acceptor as soon as we receive the Bill? Because (1) the Bill *satisfies the debt for the present*; the debt is *not legally due* till the Bill is mature. (2) If we open an account for the Acceptor, and debit it, that representation is correct only so long as we keep the Acceptance. When we part with it, the new holder of it claims the Acceptor as *his* debtor. (3) The Bill enables us to get paid earlier by the Discounter or Endorsee than by the Acceptor. When the Endorseè pays us, it would be false to credit the Acceptor's account and close it, as if the Acceptor had honoured his Bill.

These are the fundamental facts respecting Acceptances given me instead of cash by my debtors—*i.e.*, my drafts on them :—

(1) A Bill Receivable in my books is an *Asset* of mine, representing money I am to *receive*. Any Bill in my possession, not cancelled or not mature, must be a Bill Receivable. It is first entered on the Debit side (my Asset side) as received.

(2) When a Bill Receivable is mature the Bills Receivable account must be credited, to cancel the Asset on the Debit side, *no matter whether honoured or dishonoured*. The Asset changes its place; to Cash account if honoured, to Acceptor's Personal account if dishonoured.

(3) No Bill must be debited to the Acceptor's *Personal* account until dishonoured. If still in my possession, I credit Bills Receivable account and debit Acceptor's account; if already credited in Bills Receivable account because endorsed over to Smith, I must credit Smith, because I owe him what Acceptor ought to have paid him and did not.

(4) When Goods are paid for, or a debt settled, by a Bill being given me for the amount, I must consider the account closed, and my claim satisfied *until the Acceptance falls due.*

BILLS PAYABLE ACCOUNT.

A BILL Payable in my Books is *my own Acceptance*, a Draft of one of my creditors on me. It represents money *I have to pay*. It is a *Liability* of mine, and is first entered on the Cr. side. I part with the Bill instead of parting with cash, and credit Bills Payable account instead of crediting Cash account. A Bank Cheque may be considered as a Bill Payable at sight in the Banker's books. If, when I buy Goods of Wright invoiced at £80, Wright draws on me for that amount, and I give him my Acceptance for it at one month, that Bill is a Bill Payable in my books, because it is a Liability of mine. It is, however, a Bill Receivable in Wright's books, because an Asset to him. But although Wright is my creditor for £80, I open no account for Wright, because I may not have to pay Wright, but some one to whom Wright has sold the Bill; and because, *for the present*, the Bill satisfies the debt, *nothing is owing till the Bill is mature*. It is treated as a ready-money transaction; Wright gets the Bill, I the Goods, and there the matter ends for the present. When I credit Bills Payable account I write "By Goods £80," not "By Wright." Wright enters the Bill on the Dr. side of his Bills Receivable account, writing "To Goods £80." My name will not enter his Ledger unless I dishonour my Acceptance, then he will debit me and credit his Bills Receivable account. I should open an account for Wright, and credit it £80; and debit Bills Payable account, not because I receive back my Acceptance, but because the Liability goes from that account, and assumes the form of a personal debt, as a credit in Wright's account. If Wright had sold the Bill to Grover he would credit Grover £80, and debit me £80; his Bills Receivable account was credited when he parted with the Bill. I should credit Grover instead of crediting Wright. The chief points to remember about Bills Payable are:—

(1) A Bill Payable in my books is a *Liability* of mine, and first appears on the Liability or Credit side of Bills Payable account.

(2) It is a stamped written acknowledgment of debt with *my own name written across it*, and, unless honoured, is in the possession of one of my creditors.

(3) In a Balance Sheet, it goes with Liabilities, as a Bill Receivable goes with Assets.

(4) When the Bill is mature I owe the promised money to *whoever may then hold the Bill*, not necessarily to the Drawer, the original creditor.

Balances in the Bills Accounts. — In a Bills Receivable account, any Balance must be a *Debit* Balance, an Asset, showing that some Bill is not yet mature, and so not yet cancelled by a credit entry. That Bill I have by me. It represents money owing to me.

In a Bills Payable account, any Balance must be a *Credit* Balance, a Liability, showing that some Bill I have given to a creditor is still out, not yet mature, and I still owe the money. If mature, whether honoured by me or dishonoured, it would be debited in Bills Payable account. The Liability on the Credit side would be cancelled in this account, because transferred to my creditor's Personal account if dishonoured, to Cash account if honoured.

Any Bill *in my own keeping* must be a Bill Receivable ; any Bill of mine *out* must be a Bill Payable. I keep Bills Receivable ready to present to the Acceptor or Debtor when mature. My creditors keep my Bills Payable, my own Acceptances, ready to present to me for payment when mature. They have drawn on me and I have

T. P. 6

accepted their Draft, because I owe them so much money. A Banker owes a depositor the money he has deposited; the latter draws on the Bank for that amount. The depositor's draft or cheque is a Bill Payable at sight in the Banker's books. In the depositor's books it is a Bill Receivable at sight.

Caution! When I send a Bill to my Banker for collection, I must not debit the Bank with the amount of the Bill until I know that the Acceptor has honoured his acceptance. If dishonoured the Bill will be immediately returned to me. Then I debit the Defaulter, the dishonoured Acceptor.

Advantages of Bills.

1. A creditor can get his money more easily when acknowledged on a Bill. The law assists him more; the publicity of dishonour is greater; the time for payment is fixed.

2. Money can be immediately raised on a Bill, provided the Acceptor's credit is good. The creditor thus gets paid by the discounter of the Bill earlier than he would be by the Acceptor.

3. Payments can be made *in distant lands* by Bills without the trouble and risk of sending gold.

Accommodation Bills.

Unscrupulous men short of cash raise money on one another's Bills. These are called Accommodation Bills. A draws on B for £100, and B accepts the Bill though he has received no value whatever from A. A gets some one to buy B's acceptance for £98. In return for this, B draws on A for £100, and induces somebody to give him £98 for A's acceptance. Both men get cash, but by a trick which serves only for a time.

NOTES ON THE SINGLE-ENTRY SET OF ACCOUNTS WITH THEIR SUBDIVISIONS OR SUBSIDIARY ACCOUNTS.

Valuation Account.—Instead of one general Valuation account to receive all our permanent Assets, such as fixtures, implements, trade plant, business premises, horses and vans, and everything we require in our business, but do not sell for profit, we may open a separate account for each. Each must be treated exactly as the Valuation account. All lessening of the Asset on the Debit side by depreciation, loss, damage, death or sale must be credited, and the Debit Excess of each of the accounts must come as an Asset into Final Balance Sheet.

Debit Balance of Goods Account, Contract Account, Ship Account, etc. — The Debit Balance of any of the Trade accounts, showing Goods remaining unsold when books are closed; material bought, but not used, for any contract; and the value of the vessel in a Ship account, are all Final Assets for Final Balance Sheet, and so belong to the Single-Entry Set *so far as these Balances are concerned*; though the accounts themselves all have a Credit Excess to be credited to Profit and Loss, or a Debit Excess to be debited to it, and so belong to the Double-Entry Set. These balances must all be brought into the Single-Entry Set either by adding them to the Debit side of Valuation account, or opening a separate account for them—"Debit Balances of Trade accounts." Some, however, *debit them at once to Balance account*. They are credited to Trade account, or Contract account, or Ship account, as if sold at cost price, and debited to Balance account at once, without being first debited to Valuation account, or an account of their own. The disadvantage of this method is that *Trial Balance*, not having these balances included in its totals, is imperfect, and the final results cannot be got from it until these balances are added in on both sides. In reopening books, they must be debited, each to its own account, otherwise we cannot get at the profit or the loss. For a like reason, any advance or part payment beforehand for a Contract, or a Consignment Outwards, must be *credited as a Liability*, each to its own account, as explained under Trade account.

Petty Cash Account.—Sometimes a separate account is kept for trifling outlays by assistants during the chief's absence. Supposing a boy, whom we will call Petty Cash clerk, has charge of this cash. What he receives from Cashier he debits to his account; what he pays away he credits to it. The Debit balance at close shows what he still has. This is another of my Assets for Final Balance Sheet.

Consignment Inwards Account; Selling on Commission Account. — When Smith sends me a Consignment of Goods to sell for him *at his risk*, I open a Personal account for *Smith*, the Consignor, and debit it with any money I lay out on the Consignment, and with what I charge as Commission for selling. I credit it with what I get for the Goods, for the money is Smith's. The Credit Balance is what I owe Smith; it is a Liability of mine. It must be carefully noted that *I take no account at all of what Smith may invoice his Goods at.* If I get more, I shall owe him more; if less, I shall owe him less. When an Auctioneer receives a Consignment of Furniture to dispose of, Consignor may value it at £50; Consignee may realise £80, however, but then he credits £80 to Consignor's account. Should be realise but £30, he credits Consignor with but £30. *Consignee makes no profit but his commission;* he incurs no loss whatever, and does not credit Consignor's account with a penny till the Goods are sold, and *the money in.*

A del Credĕre Agent's Account.—If I sell Goods for Smith *at my own risk*, having to make good the value of all Goods sold for him, I am a *del Credere Agent*, and I charge a much larger commission. When I part with any of them to Prior, I debit Prior's account and credit Consignor's. Prior is *my* debtor, and if he fails to pay I lose. But if I sell for cash only, I am like an auctioneer. I credit Consignor's account with all I receive for his Goods, and debit him with my commission, and what I pay for carting, etc. The Credit Balance is what I owe Consignor.

When I purchase Goods for Brown on commission, I open a Personal account for Brown, and debit him with all I lay out for him, and with my commission, crediting

Cash account for the one and Profit and Loss for the other. Should Brown send me a Draft in advance, whether his own Acceptance, another man's, or a Draft on the Bank where I reside, I credit his account with the amount. The Debit Excess is what Brown owes me. It is an Asset of mine.

Mortgage Account, Mortgagee's Account.—If I borrow money on the security of my business premises, machinery, or other permanent assets, I open a Mortgagee's account, and *credit* it with what I owe him, the money lent. When the interest falls due, if I pay promptly, I debit Profit and Loss (for it is a dead loss), and credit Cash. If I do not pay I must credit Mortgagee's account, for I now owe mortgage *plus* interest. When I pay the interest, I debit Mortgagee's account and credit Cash. When I pay off any part of the mortgage I debit Mortgagee's account, as I should that of any other creditor, to cancel the Liability entered against me on the Cr. side. If, on closing Books, there is a Credit Balance, it shows *what I still owe*. It is a Liability. There cannot be a Debit Balance.

Outstanding Accounts, Liabilities or Assets.— Sometimes, on closing Books, there are several little accounts just fallen due to me, but not yet paid : outstanding Assets. A separate account for each need not be opened, but one general " Outstanding Assets account," which must be *debited* with what is owing to me just as I debit any ordinary Debtor's account. It is a Sundry Debtors' account. When they pay I debit Cash and credit this account, thus cancelling the Asset, because gone form this account. When there are such accounts as gas, rates, rent, wages, etc., just fallen due, but which *I still owe*, all may be collected together in one Outstanding Liabilities account, which must be *credited* with what I owe, just as any other Creditor's account is. When I pay them, Cash account is credited, and this account debited, to cancel the Liability.

Cautions!—

1. Never bring into Cash account anything but cash *actually received* or *actually paid away*.

2. Whenever cash is paid out of the business, and nothing tangible is received in return for it, Profit and Loss must be debited. But if anything remains to show for it, such as office furniture, permanent improvements to shop, or addition to fixtures, *Valuation account* must be debited. The asset has not disappeared, is not lost to me, but exists in another form, and appears in another account. Whenever money comes in without any having gone out to get it, as from interest paid me, commission or discount allowed me, Profit and Loss must be credited to increase Capital.

3. The value of *Goods left unsold* and credited to Trade account *as if sold*, the money spent on any *open Contract* or any *open Consignment Outwards* or *Joint Adventure*, all these are *Final Assets* for Final Balance Sheet. They are moneys spent on Goods not yet sold, and represent Assets either in my own possession or sent to my customers and not yet paid for. They rank as my Assets, being amounts due to me. They resemble Goods account with the Cr. side missing, goods bought but not yet sold. Every Trade

account, unless everything belonging to it is sold up, must have a Balance for Final Balance Sheet, as well as an Excess of Profit or Loss for Profit and Loss account.

NOTES ON THE DOUBLE-ENTRY SET OF ACCOUNTS WITH THEIR SUBDIVISIONS OR SUBSIDIARY ACCOUNTS.

WHENEVER a pupil meets with an unfamiliar account, he must ask himself "Are these transactions like those of a Goods account, my outlay on the Dr. side, my receipts or returns for that outlay on the Cr. side, and the *Cr. Excess* showing Profit or increase to Capital?" If so, it is one of the Trade accounts, and must be treated just the same. Its credit excess must go to the Credit side of Profit and Loss; and if any goods remain over unsold, or any outlays not settled up, these are *Assets* for Final Balance Sheet, and must be taken away to it, or first passed through Valuation account on its way to it. Every Trade account belongs to *both* sets of accounts unless all the goods are sold out.

But if the transactions yield me *no profit except commission for buying and selling*, as in Selling on Commission acccunts and Purchasing on Commission accounts,—if they yield me profit only *incidentally*, as when I buy for £390 cash a Bill for £400,—these, when not Bills account, are *personal accounts*, my customers' accounts in my books. Credit Balances here are liabilities of mine, and show what I owe them. These accounts belong to the Single-Entry Set, as before explained.

In the Ledgers of large mercantile houses, all the accounts are very much subdivided, both Sets alike. In the Single-Entry Set there are separate accounts opened for (1) Premises, (2) Fixtures, (3) Plant, (4) Horses, (5) Office furniture, etc. The Double-Entry Accounts are still more minutely divided up. But when the learner finds a special account opened for Wages and Salaries, he knows this is a part of the Dr. side of Profit and Loss; if a separate account for Commissions Paid to the Firm, he knows this is a part of the Cr. side of Profit and Loss; and so with the rest.

Partners' Accounts, Current Accounts.—Where there are several Partners, a separate Capital account is opened for each, and a Current account for each too. The Current account is a part of the Capital account, and opened only to keep the latter free from details. Both are *the Personal accounts* of the Owners of the business. Each Partner is credited with what he lends to the business; *i.e.* on the Cr. side of A's Capital account is entered A's share of the Firm's Capital. All other entries affecting A are made in A's Current account. If he adds to his Capital by an advance or loan to the Firm, his Current account is credited with it; the interest charged against Profits on his Capital, and his share of Profit at close, are also credited to it. But if he withdraws money from the business, or takes Goods out of Stock for his private use, his Current account is *debited* with what he *receives*. It is also debited with interest charged on the amounts withdrawn. This is a gain to the Firm (and is credited to Profit and Loss account), though a loss to him. On closing Books, the Credit Excess of A's Current account is taken to the Credit of his Capital account; and the resulting Credit Excess of A's Capital account, showing what the Firm owes to A, is just what would have been obtained if the entries on the Credit side of Current account had been made at once in Capital account, and what has been debited to Current account had been debited to Capital account at once. Specimen Current and Capital accounts are given at the end of the Practical Part. If there are four Partners, A, B, C, & D, the Final Net Capital of all four added together must agree with the Excess of Assets over Liabilities in the Single-Entry Set. These four accounts collectively represent the Capital account in an ordinary Ledger.

Subdivisions oi Profit and Loss Account.— Sometimes an account is opened specially for Trade Expenses, another for Discounts allowed by the Firm, a third for Commissions paid by them, a fourth for Bad Debts. These are nothing but the Debit or Loss side of Profit and Loss account. A fifth account shows Discounts received by the Firm, a sixth Commissions received by them, a seventh Interest received by them on overdue accounts and from money lent to Banker and others. These are the Credit side of Profit and Loss account. Each must be balanced and closed when the Ledger is closed, and Debit Excesses, as dead losses, taken to the Debit side of Profit and Loss account; and Credit Excesses, as clear profit, taken to the Credit side of Profit and Loss account. This account, then, represents the resultant or combined effect of all the gains and losses summarised from its various subsidiary accounts. To summarise readily, all the subsidiaries should come together, and immediately after their principal account, just as all the subdivisions of Capital account, each Partner's Capital account followed by his Current account, come together at the commencement of the Ledger. Bad Debts Reserve Fund and Repairs Reserve Fund are explained in an article of their own.

Subdivisions of Trade or Goods Account.—A farmer may keep his Dairy account apart from his Corn account, and have two Trade accounts. A country dealer may sell grocery, drapery, and shoes, and keep three separate Trade accounts. A merchant may have one account for tea, another for coffee, a third for cocoa, a fourth for spices, a fifth for sugar. Each of these must be treated as an ordinary Goods account. Usually there is a Credit Excess showing profit in each; and also *a Debit Balance of Goods left unsold at close.* The *Credit Excess* of each must be taken to the Credit side of Profit and Loss to increase Capital. But *the value of Goods on hand* in each must, as a Final Asset, go into Final Balance Sheet.

Contract Accounts. — These are Trade accounts, showing on Dr. side all amounts I spend on wages, architect's fees, materials and cartage; on the other, all advances made to me and final payments received by me. The Credit Excess is Profit to be taken to the Credit side of Profit and Loss. *Nothing here must be debited to Profit and Loss,* because every penny I lay out in wages, etc., will come back to me in what I receive, and I shall not know what I gain on the contract unless I debit to it every expense incurred. *Should any material remain unused,* these are like Goods on hand, and must come as an Asset into Final Balance Sheet. And if, on reopening Books, there is any balance of unused materials left from an old Closed Contract, or if money has been spent on labour or materials on a new *Open* Contract, these are Assets just like Goods on hand at commencement, and must be debited to the new Open Contract. When there are several Contracts each must bear a distinctive number or name, and must be separately balanced. Where there is a Credit Excess showing profit, it is carried to the Credit side of Profit and Loss; where there is a Debit Excess showing loss, that is carried to the Debit side of Profit and Loss. The value of unused materials remaining is an Asset for Final Balance Sheet, as before explained.

Consignments Outwards.—When I send to Mann, of Hamburg, a Consignment of Goods for him to sell *on my account* and *at my risk*, I open a Consignment Outwards account, and debit it with all I lay out on it. If I put any of my own stock of Goods into it, I credit Goods account, and debit this. If I pay away money on freightage, dock dues, or Goods purchased for it, I credit Cash and debit Consignment Outwards. When I receive from Mann his *Account Sales*, showing what he has realised by selling my Consignment, after paying his own commission and charges, I credit the Consignment with the amount realised, and debit Mann's Personal account. When Mann pays, I credit Mann and debit Cashier. The Credit Excess, if any, is my clear profit on the Consignment, and goes to the Credit side of Profit and Loss. Should Mann, in his Account Sales, state that any Goods remain over unsold, their value is an Asset for Final Balance Sheet. And on reopening Books, if any such remainder is spoken of, it is an Asset to be debited to Consignment Outwards account, forming a part of my next Consignment to Mann.

Ship Account.—If a fishmonger has a smack, and uses it for fishing purposes, he may enter its value in Valuation account, and write off something for depreciation at the year's end. But if a merchant or a shipping company have vessels built, equip them, put a cargo on board, insure them, pay captain and crew to navigate them, and dock dues and harbour dues for their safety, a Ship account must be opened, and debited with all these and any other outlay. On the Credit side must be entered what passengers pay, what is paid as freightage for merchandise taken out for other people, and the net proceeds of the sale of cargo. The Credit Excess is profit to go on Credit side of Profit and Loss. But before balancing Ship account, the value of the vessel at the time of closing Books must be credited to this account, and debited to Valuation account as an Asset for Final Balance Sheet. It is another Goods account, and the value of the vessel corresponds to that of Goods left unsold.

Investment Account: Consols, Railway Shares, etc.; House Property.

If, instead of buying Goods, I use some of my money in buying up Railway Shares, Corporation Stock, or House

Property, buying when cheap and selling when dear, I must treat these transactions as another Trade affair. All I lay out on the property, including repairs to houses, I debit to Investment account, and credit to Cash. All that comes in, dividends or interest, or rent, or money received on sales, must be credited to Investment account. Nothing goes to Profit and Loss until the excess is found. If there is a Credit Excess, it goes as profit to the Credit side of Profit and Loss; if a Debit Excess, to the Debit side of Profit and Loss as a loss. But before balancing, the value of all shares still in possession, at current price, must be credited to Investment account, as if sold, and debited to Valuation account as an Asset for Final Balance Sheet.

But if the houses are bought *not to sell again*, but simply to save rent, or to get rent as interest on the money laid out; if the shares are bought only for the interest, no Investment account should be opened. Valuation account must be debited, and Cash credited with the outlay, and the shares or house property treated as permanent Assets. When rent or interest is received, this, being clear gain, is credited to Profit and Loss and debited to Cash.

At the close of the year, if the shares have gone up in value Valuation account should be debited with the increase; the depreciation for wear and tear of the house must be credited. This is one of the Single-Entry Set. The Debit Balance goes to Final Balance Sheet as an Asset. It is property in actual possession.

Joint Speculation Account; Joint Adventure Account.

Sometimes a merchant, in addition to his ordinary business, enters on a speculation with others to share the risks or to divide the profits from this one adventure only. Suppose I think money can be made by a shipment of Goods to Rio Janeiro, and four others join me in this venture, each paying one-fifth of the outlay, and each receiving one-fifth of the net proceeds. I open four Personal accounts for my four co-speculators, and a *Joint Adventure account* for myself, the Personal accounts among the Single-Entry Set, the Joint Adventure account among the Double-Entry accounts as a Trade account. This last I must treat as a Goods account, a part of my own Personal account. Let us call my co-adventurers A, B, C, and D. If I find the Goods (£1000 worth), I credit Goods account £1000 as sold to the adventure, and debit Joint Adventure £200, and A, B, C, and D each with £200. If A furnishes them, I credit A's account £1000, and debit as before. Whatever other expenses are incurred must be credited to Cash if paid by me, but credited to C if paid by C. They must be debited to the five accounts, one-fifth to each as before. If I have the management of the affair, and charge commission on all outlay, I credit Profit and Loss, and debit one-fifth of it to each of the five accounts. If D has the management of it, and is to be paid commission, but has not received it, D's account must be credited instead of Profit and Loss. If I pay D, I credit

Cash and debit each adventurer's account one-fifth. D must not be debited with the whole, unless first credited with it. If B pays £5 dock dues for it, B must be credited £5, and each of the five accounts debited £1. When the Account Sales is received showing the *net* proceeds, say £2000, Consignee at Rio Janeiro must be debited £2000, and each of the five credited with £400. If the cargo were insured for £2000 and lost at sea, the underwriters would be debited £2000, as if they had bought the cargo for that sum. On balancing these five accounts, there will be the same Credit Balance of Profit for each of the co-adventurers; but in the accounts of A, B, C, and D they are *Liabilities* of mine—they show amounts which I owe them. In my own account—"Joint Adventure account"—the Credit Balance is *my own Profit*, to be carried away to the Credit side of Profit and Loss. The learner must note that in debiting Consignee or Underwriters, I enter them as *my* debtors for the whole amount. When they pay me the £2000, I debit Cashier's account, and credit Consignees or Underwriters. I now have the whole of the proceeds, and owe my co-adventurers their shares. Had the proceeds been paid to A, neither Consignee nor Underwriters would have been debited in my books, but A would have been debited £2000. This would have given a *Debit* balance in A's account, due to me. In closing Books, then, A's balance would have been an Asset of mine; B's, C's, and D's balances, Liabilities. The Credit Excess of my own account—"Joint Adventure account"—does not come into Balance Sheet, but goes as profit to the Credit side of Profit and

Loss; for the account belongs to the Double-Entry Set, whereas the Personal accounts belong to the Single-Entry Set.

The Order in which the Ledger Accounts should come.

All the Trade accounts, including Ship account, Consignment Outwards, and Joint Adventure account, must come together, and immediately follow Profit and Loss account, which receives the excess from each, either as profit on its Credit side or as loss on its Debit side. The learner should open the accounts always in the following order, omitting any not wanted in an exercise, but preserving the same sequence :—

Double-Entry Set.
- A's Capital account.
- A's Current account.
- B's Capital account.
- B's Current account.
- Profit and Loss account.
- Subsidiary Profit and Loss accounts.
- Trade account.
- Subsidiary Trade accounts.

Single-Entry Set.
- Valuation account (including Goods left in Trade accounts).
- Subsidiary Valuation accounts.
- Bank account.
- Cash account.
- Petty Cash account.
- Bills Receivable account.
- Bills Payable account.
- Personal accounts.
- Reserve Fund account.
- Outstanding Assets account.
- Outstanding Liabilities account.

The learner is recommended to begin, when closing Books, with the Trade accounts, and to carry the Goods on hand, left unsold, from each of them, to the debit side of Valuation account, and to include them in Trial Balance. They will not then be forgotten, as they often are. On reopening Books, they must be debited each to its own Trade account.

Reserve Fund Account: Future Bad-Debt Fund. Repairs-Reserve Fund (one of the Single-Entry Set).

Sometimes a Company sets aside £10,000 as a Reserve Fund to meet extraordinary expenses not yet incurred, but possible. A shopkeeper, bound by his lease to repaint his premises every three years at a cost of £60, sets that amount aside as a Reserve Fund. Sometimes a firm sets aside £300 yearly as a provision for *Future* Bad Debts. An account is opened below the personal accounts and headed " Reserve Fund." The amount set aside is *credited* to this account, just as it would if the firm actually owed this amount to some customer. It is entered as a future *liability*, as I might enter £500 to the credit of my Banker's account, if the Banker had discounted Bills Receivable for me to that amount, and the Bills not being yet mature, the Acceptors may dishonour them, and in that case I should have to pay the Banker back. Here, however, when crediting Banker I debit Acceptors; whereas the amount credited to a Reserve Fund must be debited to Profit and Loss as a dead loss, or lessening of Capital. I consider the money *gone*, and in dividing profits, treat it as due to some customer. If a Railway Company sets aside £50,000 as a Reserve, the effect of that will be that there will be £50,000 less profit to be divided among partners or shareholders, because in their Final Balance Sheet the Reserve appears as a Liability, and so lessens what remains to be shared. If I write off £60 as a Repairs-Reserve Fund, I debit Profit and Loss account £60, as I should if my horse, worth £60, died, or a debtor of mine, owing me £60, absconded; I credit Reserve Fund £60. If the repairs, when executed, cost me £90, I must not debit Reserve Fund £90. If I did, there would be a Debit Balance of £30, and a Debit Balance must show an Asset of mine. How can this £30 represent an Asset of mine, when it means *I owe* that amount over and above what I have made provision for in my Reserve Fund? I must debit Profit and Loss £30 to show I lose another £30; I must debit Reserve Fund account £60 to cancel the Liability, as it no longer exists. If I pay the painter promptly, his account does not enter my books at all. It is a ready-money transaction, just as paying rent, wages, or receiving commission on goods sold for a consignor. I credit Cash £90 if paid; if not paid, I credit an account opened for the painter. In either case, I debit Profit and Loss £30, and debit Reserve Fund £60. Reserve Fund is now closed. No Liability exists in it, but I have £60 less in Cashier's keeping: nay, £90 less; in Profit and Loss account £60 has been already debited when Reserve Fund was opened, and it must be debited with another £30, because Capital is diminished by £90. Whenever a diminution of Capital takes place—

a dead loss, that is—both sets of accounts must show the lessening.

Balance in the Reserve Fund.

Any Balance in a Reserve Fund, just as in a Bills Payable account, must be a *Credit Balance*, showing a part of the Liability not yet met, a portion of the outlay provided for not yet paid. So also in a Bad-Debt Reserve Fund. There cannot be a Debit Balance. (See APPENDIX, Note 1.)

Loan Account: My Debtor's Personal Account (one of the Single-Entry Set).

If I lend money on interest, I open an account for the borrower and debit it. When he pays interest, I debit the cash received to Cash account, and credit Profit and Loss. The interest is clear *gain* to me. But if borrower neglects to pay, he owes me the interest now, and must be debited with that too. When he pays it I credit his account, and debit Cash account. When he repays any part of the sum borrowed I credit him, and debit Cash, as before. Any balance there may be at close must be *a Debit Balance*, showing what is still owing to me, an Asset of mine. The learner must carefully note that borrower's account is *not* credited when he pays interest, unless first debited with it. If he borrowed £100 and paid £5 interest, that payment would not lessen the amount due: £100 would still be owing. But if £5 were credited to borrower, the balance left due would be but £95. The account to be credited is my own Profit and Loss account. It increases what the business owes me.

CONSIGNMENT OUTWARDS (a Trade Account belonging to the Double-Entry Set).

CONSIGNMENT INWARDS (a Personal Account belonging to the Single-Entry Set).

THE beginner must carefully distinguish between (1) a Consignment of Goods which I send away for another to sell *on my account* and *at my risk*, and (2) a Consignment Inwards received by me to sell for another *at his risk*. The former, the Consignment Outwards, is in my Books, a Trade account ; the latter simply the Personal account of the Consignor.

An Open Consignment-Outwards Balance.

If, on closing Books, the net proceeds of the sale of the Consignment are not known, and the Consignment cannot therefore be balanced and closed, it must be treated as an *Open Contract account*, or a Goods account with the Credit or Selling side wanting. The Debit side represents Goods bought but not yet sold—an Asset for Final Balance Sheet. The total amount debited must be taken to the Debit side of Valuation account, or to the Debit side of an account opened for it among the Single-Entry Set. Some transfer it at once to the Debit side of Balance account, as the double entry of the equalising amount on the Credit side of Open Consignment Outwards account. It must be dealt with as Goods on hand at close are. On reopening Books, it must take its old place on the Debit side of Consignment Outwards account.

Cautions !

1. When a Consignment is sent off, do not debit the

Consignee with the value, but debit Consignment Outwards account. Debit the Consignee when you know what he has received for you on the sales. Think of an auctioneer selling furniture for you.

2. When a Consignment comes in do not credit Consignor till you have received money for him. Debit him if you spend money for him. For the same reason Banker must not be debited when I send him Bills Receivable to collect. I must wait to see if any are dishonoured, for he will not get the money for these, and I shall be the loser, not he.

OMITTED TRANSACTIONS.

Transactions with Persons not recorded in those Persons' Accounts at all. Transactions omitted from other Accounts.

1. *No ready-money business is recorded in any personal account* (*i.e.* in no account headed with a person's name). If I buy Goods of Jones for £10, cash down, my Goods account receives a debit, my Cash account a credit, of £10; for both these accounts are *altered* by the transaction. But if I had an account for Jones in my Ledger, and entered this transaction, I should debit him £10 for the money he receives, and credit him £10 for the goods he parts with, and both transactions being simultaneous, and the values given and received equal, his account is not altered, and both entries are therefore omitted. When rent *is paid, as soon as due,* to landlord, wages to servants, salary to clerk, rates and taxes to collector, premium to

fire insurance company, and so on, all these are ready money transactions; Profit and Loss is debited, Cash credited. The person who receives the money must never be debited, unless first credited. Debiting Landlord would make him owe me the rent! When Coombs, one of two partners, is paid, besides profits, a fixed salary of £100 a year, as a first charge on profits, *if he draws it out when due*, this, too, is a ready-money transaction, and does not come into Coombs' Personal or Capital account at all. It is credited to Cash and debited to Profit and Loss, as a clerk's salary is. It is not debited to Coombs. If it were, it would mean that Coombs had withdrawn £100 from his Capital, and therefore had £100 less to receive from his business; whereas his Capital remains untouched. If he does not draw it out, he must be credited with it, instead of Cash account being credited.

2. When *Bills* are given instead of Cash, the transaction is not recorded in the Personal account of Acceptor or Drawer, but is regarded as a ready-money transaction *until the Bill has matured*. If Newman sells me Goods £200, and I give him my Acceptance for £200 at three months, although I owe Newman £200, I do not consider any *person* as my creditor till the three months have expired, because my creditor then may not be Newman, but X, the then holder of my Acceptance. Meanwhile, I consider Newman paid, because he has my Bill, *which he can sell.* So, when I sell Goods, £50, to Smith, and draw on him, Smith having given me his Acceptance, *which I can sell*, I consider Smith to have paid me, *for the present,* much in the same way as if he had given me a horse or

other saleable asset for my Goods. I do not debit Smith, because I may get paid before it is time for Smith to pay me. The Bill debited in Bills Receivable account I consider as much an Asset as a horse debited to Valuation account as worth £50. Having this, I consider Smith's account closed for the present. Hence, if Jarvis buys goods of me worth £80, and gives me a Bill for £50, I debit Jarvis's account with £30 only. I credit Goods account £80 ; debit £50 to Bills Receivable, and debit £30 to Jarvis ; £50 is considered paid, for the present.

3. When A requests B to pay C £50 for D, D opens accounts only for A whom he credits £50, and for C whom he debits £50. (See CYCLICAL TRANSACTIONS.)

4. When Goods worth £5 are lost, damaged, or taken from Stock as samples, Profit and Loss should be debited £5, and Goods credited £5, as if sold for nothing. But we *may* omit both entries altogether. For when Goods left unsold are valued, they will be worth £5 less; consequently £5 less will be credited to Goods account, and also £5 less debited to Valuation account as a Final Asset. Now the £5 omitted on the Credit side of Goods account will give £5 less profit on the Goods, when we make no entry at the time of the loss; but then there is no loss entered on the Debit side of Profit and Loss because the loss is evident in the diminished valuation. When we credit Goods £5, and debit Profit and Loss £5 at the time, there is £5 more profit on Goods; but this is neutralised by the £5 loss debited in Profit and Loss. The two results are the same. Capital is lessened £5 ; we have £5 worth less of Goods on hand. No entry is

absolutely necessary, but it is better to make it at the time. When Goods are taken for private use, they must be debited to Capital account, and not to Profit and Loss, as if used in the business. They should at once be credited to Goods account, because to credit them as if sold to a customer gives a truer account of Trade Profit.

5. Hughes of Madras owes me £500, and I owe Gibson of Madras £500. I draw on Hughes for £500, favour of Gibson, and send it to Gibson. He will take it to Hughes for his Acceptance, and keep it till mature, or sell it. Hughes will pay Gibson, if Gibson has not parted with the Bill, when the time named on it expires. This transaction does not enter my Bills Receivable account at all, though a Bill Receivable is concerned. It does not, because, if recorded, *the account would remain unaltered as to balance.* The two accounts altered are Hughes's and Gibson's. I credit Hughes and debit Gibson.

6. "Seymour, a creditor of mine, asks me to remit him £200 in Bills on New Orleans, at ten days' sight. I do so, purchasing the same at Bank." Here I no sooner get the Bills than I part with them at the same price, and Bills Receivable account is not affected as to balance. I debit Seymour £200 and credit Bank £200.

7. If I begin business with £700 borrowed from Draper, Capital account need receive no entry. The Cash Asset of £700 being neutralised by the Liability of £700 due to Draper, I call my Initial Net Capital nil, and make no entry in it.

8. When Adams sends me a Consignment of Goods invoiced at £150 to sell for him at his risk, I must not credit Adams one penny till I have sold his Goods. I then owe him the Net Proceeds, and credit him accordingly.

9. When I consign Goods for another to sell at my risk, I do not debit Consignee one penny till I hear what he has cleared by selling them. I then debit him with the Net Proceeds.

CYCLICAL OR ROUNDABOUT TRANSACTIONS.

Payments we make on Account of Others effected by Booking.

EXAMPLE 1.—Bach, through his Banker, pays £500 to Chard for Drake at request of Abb. There is no transference of cash from Banker to Chard. Bach and Chard have the same Banker. Give the various entries made by each of the five men in his own Journal.

> *In Bach's Journal.* £500 Abb Dr.
> To Bank Cr. £500.

Bach debits Abb because the money is paid at Abb's request to Abb's nominee, and Bach will look to Abb for repayment. Bach's Banking account is affected adversely, £500 being paid out of it into Chard's account.

> *In Banker's Journal.* £500 Bach Dr.
> To Chard Cr. £500.

Banker pays the money out of Bach's account into Chard's account. Bach's Credit balance in the Banker's books is diminished, Chard's increased. Banker owes Chard £500 more.

In Drake's Journal. £500 Chard Dr.
> To Abb Cr. £500.

When Drake learns that Chard's account has been credited £500 at the Bank on *his* account, he acts just as he would if he heard that £500 cash had been lodged with Chard to deliver to him. If he is not at once paid, he debits Chard's account £500. As he is indebted to Abb for it, he credits Abb, just as he would if Abb himself handed him £500.

In Chard's Journal. £500 Bank Dr.
> To Drake Cr. £500.

The £500 credited to Chard in Banker's book is Drake's property, and must be credited to him in Chard's book. This new Liability of Chard's will be just met when Chard debits his Bank account £500, for the £500 placed to his Credit in Banker's books Chard owes Drake.

In Abb's Journal. £500 Drake Dr.
> To Bach Cr. £500.

As Drake has virtually received £500 by being so credited in Chard's books, and receives it at Abb's request, Abb debits Drake. He credits Bach because Bach has paid through his Banker £500 to Chard.

The actual money will change hands when these men settle their accounts with each other.

EXAMPLE 2.—Arch asks Bryce to pay £5 cash to Coombs for Duke. How is this transaction posted in these four men's Ledgers, supposing the only passing of money to be from Bryce to Coombs?

Arch owes Duke £5. He pays him by getting Bryce to pay £5 to Coombs, cash changing hands.

In Arch's Ledger.—Arch debits Duke £5 and credits Bryce £5. He debits Duke, because he will look to him to make good what Arch will owe Bryce. Instead of owing £5 to Duke, he now owes it to Bryce.

In Bryce's Ledger.—Bryce debits Arch, and credits his own Cash account. He would have credited Coombs if he had not actually paid him. Instead of £5 in his cash box, there is a debt of £5 due to him from Arch.

In Coombs' Ledger.—Coombs debits Cash and credits Duke. He has £5 more in his cash box, but it belongs to Duke. He owes it to him.

In Duke's Ledger.—Duke debits Coombs and credits Arch. When Duke hears that Coombs has received money on his account, he books Coombs as his debtor for the amount. He knows it came really from Arch, and credits him, as if Arch himself paid him £5.

Summary.—Arch now owes Bryce £5 instead of owing Duke £5. Bryce has a debt of £5 due to him from Arch. Coombs owes Duke £5, which he received from Bryce. Duke has £5 due to him from Coombs instead of from Arch.

EXAMPLE 3.—I am instructed by Mason to deliver coals worth £10 to Wood. How does this transaction appear in our three Ledgers?

In my Ledger, I debit Mason £10 and credit Coals account £10. I do not debit Wood, the receiver; I act upon orders from Mason, and look to Mason for payment.

Mason, in his Ledger, debits Wood £10, and credits my account £10. He owes me for the coals; Wood owes him for them.

Wood, in his Ledger, debits his Coals account £10, and credits Mason £10. If not a coal merchant, he would debit Profit and Loss, for a trade expense; debit Capital, if for private use. My account does not enter into Wood's books, because I act for Mason.

LEDGER ABSTRACTS, AND TRIAL BALANCE.

Debtors' and Creditors' Accounts Omitted.

EXAMPLE 1.—The part of my Ledger containing the Personal accounts has been burnt. The following balances being left visible, ascertain from them the excess of what I owe my customers over what they owe me, or *vice versa* :—

Cash, £20; Valuation, £300; Bank (overdrawn), £1; Goods, Dr., £308; Cr., £382; Profit and Loss, Dr., £1; Capital, Cr., £808. Goods on hand valued at £150 are not included in the above.

Dr	TRIAL BALANCE.		Cr
£		£	
—	Capital ...	808	Excess of Credits, i.e. of Initial Capital, plus Profits over Losses. £1,031 (d.)
1	Profit and Loss	—	
308	Trade or Goods	532	
450	Valuation ...	—	
—	Bank ...	1	
20	Cash ...	—	
?	Debtors ...	—	
--	Creditors ...	?	

Excess of Debits, i.e. of Assets over Liabilities. £469 (c.)

(a) £779   (b) £1,341

We first add value of Goods on hand to the credit side of Goods account as if sold, and to the Debit side of Valuation account as a Final Asset. When the missing items shown by the two notes of interrogation are supplied, the totals (a) and (b) will be alike; so also the excesses (c) and (d) will be alike. The difference in each case—viz., 1341—779, or 1031—469'= 562. This deficiency is on the Asset or Debit side. Hence my customers owe me £562 over and above what I owe them. This result may be obtained by the following reasoning, which, however, is only another way of putting the same thing.

The Double-Entry Set is complete. From Trade account there is a Gross Profit of £532—£308=£224. From Profit and Loss there is a Net Profit of £224 —£1=£223. From Capital account we get Final Net Capital £223+£808=£1031.

The Single-Entry Set is incomplete. The Assets given are Valuation £450, Cash £20: total £470. Liabilities £1. Excess of Assets over Liabilities £470—£1=£469. But, as seen in Double-Entry Set, this excess must be

£1031. There is missing £1031 − £469 = £562. My customers must owe me £562 over and above what I owe them. If we supply £562 on the debit side of Debtors' account, or put any two numbers where the notes of interrogation are, which give an excess of £562 to the debit side, both Sets will agree. They will show the same Grand Total both sides, and the same Final Net Capital, £1031.

Profit and Loss Account Omitted.

EXAMPLE 2.—Prepare a Profit and Loss Sheet from the following Balances in my Ledger on Dec. 31st :—
Valuation, £80; Cash, £735; Andrews, Cr., £50; Watts, Dr., £15; Goods, Dr., £115, Cr., £215; Capital, Cr., £700. Goods on hand £10 are not included in the above.

By crediting value of Goods on hand to Goods account, as if sold, and debiting them to Valuation account as a Final Asset, we get a *perfect Trial Balance*, from which we can take out any of the final results as easily as by closing the Ledger. The Balances of Valuation and Cash accounts are necessarily Debit Balances, Assets.

Dr.		TRIAL BALANCE.		Cr.
	£		£	
	——	Capital ...	700	Excess of Credits, i.e. Net Capital, plus Profits over Losses. £810 (d.)
	?	Profit and Loss	?	
	115	Goods ...	225	
Excess of Debits, i.e. of Assets over Liabilities, £790 (c.)	90	Valuation ...	——	
	735	Cash ...	——	
	——	Andrews ...	50	
	15	Watts ...	—	
(a)	£955		(b) £975	

From the Single-Entry Set, which is complete, we see the Assets exceed the Liabilities by £790. From the incomplete Double-Entry Set we see Final Net Capital appears as £810. The same difference of £20 appears in the totals (a) and (b). The disagreement is due to the omission of £20 loss on the debit side of Profit and Loss. The Gross Profit on Goods is £225 − £115 = £110. If there were no other profits, nor any losses, Final Capital would be £700 + £110 = £810. But the actual Assets, as seen in the Single-Entry Set, exceed the Liabilities by £790 only. The missing £20 shows a loss which should have gone on the Dr. side of Profit and Loss. The same final result, however, would be given by a gain of £30 credited, and £50 debited; of £5 credited, and £25 debited, etc.

Dr.   PROFIT AND LOSS SHEET.   Cr.

Losses.	£	Gains.	£
To Sundries (omitted) ...	20	By Goods, Gross Profit ...	110
„ Capital, Net Profit ...	90		
	110		110
		Net Profit	£90

EXAMPLE 3.—Open Ledger accounts for the undermentioned, post into them the given totals, close the Ledger, and ascertain (1) Net Gain, (2) Final Net Capital, (3) Final Balance Sheet. The value of Goods on hand, £129, is not included in the credits of Merchandise account, but must be credited by you to that account as if sold, and debited to Valuation account as a Final Asset.

The Dr. side of Cash is £454, Cr. side £142; Profit and Loss, Dr., £34, Cr., £2; Bank, Dr., £452, Cr., £25;

Capital, Cr., £1200; Valuation, Dr., £629; Goods, Dr., £97, Cr., £168. Begin with Merchandise, and carry balances up.

Dr. **CAPITAL ACCOUNT.** Cr.

To Balance, Final Net Capital	£1,368	By Sundries £1,200	
		,, P. & L., Net Gain... 168	
			1,368
		Final Net Capital £1,368	

Dr. **PROFIT AND LOSS ACCOUNT.** Cr.

Losses.	£	Gains.	£
To Sundries...	34	By Sundries	2
,, Capital, Net Profit ...	168	,, Merchandise, Gross Profit	200
	£202		£202
		Net Profit	£168

Dr. **MERCHANDISE ACCOUNT.** Cr.

Buying side.	£	Selling side.	£
To Sundries	97	By Sundries	168
,, Profit and Loss, Gross Profit	200	,, Valuation Account, (Goods on hand)	129
	297		297
		Gross Profit	£200

Dr. **VALUATION ACCOUNT.** Cr.

To Sundries £500	Balance £629		
,, Goods (on hand) ... 129			
£629			

Balance brought down, £629.

T. P.

8

Dr.   BANK ACCOUNT.   Cr.

To Sundries £452	By Sundries £25
	„ Balance 427
	£452

Balance brought down. £427.

Dr.   CASH ACCOUNT.   Cr.

To Sundries £454	By Sundries £142
	„ Balance 312
	£454

Balance brought down, £312.

Dr.   FINAL BALANCE SHEET.   Cr.

Liabilities.		Assets.		
Balance, Final Net } Capital	£1,368	Valuation £629
		Bank 427
		Cash 312
		£1,368

Final Net Capital £1,368

Net Gain, Credit Balance of Profit and Loss, £168.

CONSTRUCTING A POSSIBLE AND REASONABLE TRIAL BALANCE.

EXAMINERS sometimes ask candidates to draw up a supposed Trial Balance, and take out from it the final results. In doing this, the following points must be attended to, or the final results may be absurd.

1. In Valuation, Cash, and Bills Receivable, if there is any Balance, it must be a *Debit* Balance. A Credit Balance is simply impossible.

2. In Bills Payable and Reserve Fund account, if there is any Balance, it must be a *Credit* Balance.

3. The figures must be such that the totals on both sides are equal; and the Credit Excess in the Double-Entry Set must just equal the Debit Excess in the Single-Entry Set.

EXERCISE 1.—Make out a reasonable Trial Balance to include the following accounts, and compile from it (1) a Balance Sheet, (2) a Profit and Loss account, (3) a Capital account. Profits to be shared in same ratio as Capital.

Sales.	Reserve Fund.	Consignment Outwards.
Purchases.	Sundry Debtors.	Cash Inwards.
Stock-in-Trade.	Joint Adventure.	Cash Outwards.
Bank account (Not to be overdrawn).	Consignment Inwards.	Doe's Capital account.
	Profit and Loss.	Ship account.
Sundry Creditors.	Ryan's Capital account.	Trade account.

We arrange them in Double-Entry Set, and Single-Entry Set. Sales = Credit side of Trade account; Purchases = Debit side. My part of Joint Adventure is a Trade account; my co-adventurers' accounts will be included either in Creditors' or Debtors' accounts. Consignment Outwards and Ship account are Trade accounts. Stock in Trade = Balance of Goods left unsold, Valuation account. Consignment Inwards is Consignor's Personal account.

Dr.   TRIAL BALANCE.   Cr.

£		£	
80	Ryan's Capital	400	⎫ Excess of Credits, i.e., Capital + Profits over Losses, £2,600.
120	Doe's Capital	800	
350	Profit and Loss	50	
1,200	Trade or Goods	1,800	
250	Joint Adventure	350	
560	Consignment Outwards .	760	
2,750	Ship Account	3,750	⎭

£		£	
Excess of Debits, i.e., of Assets over Liabilities, £2,600. ⎧	100	Stock in Trade (valuation)	10 ⎫
	3,600	Bank	2,600
	1,200	Cash	100
	700	Sundry Debtors	— ⎬
	—	Sundry Creditors... ...	90
	400	Consignor's Account ...	500
⎩	—	Reserve Fund Account ...	100 ⎭

£11,310   £11,310

FINAL BALANCE SHEET.

Liabilities.			£	*Assets.*			£
Creditors ...	...	...	90	Valuation ...	...	...	90
Consignor ...	...	...	100	Bank	...	...	1,000
Reserve Fund	...	...	100	Cash	...	...	1,100
Balance, Final Net				Debtors	...	...	700
Capital ...	...	...	2,600				
			£2,890				£2,890

Final Net Capital £2,600.
Ryan's   ,,   ,, £853 6 8 ⎫
Doe's   ,,   ,, £1,746 13 4 ⎭

Dr.   PROFIT AND LOSS SHEET.   Cr.

Losses.	£	Gains.	£
To Sundries	350	By Sundries	50
To Capital, Net Profit...	1,600	„ Joint Adventure (profit)	100
		„ Trade (profit)	600
		„ Consignment Outward	
		(profit)	200
		„ Ship Account (profit) ...	1,000
	£1,950		£1,950
		Net Profit ...	£1,600

Dr.   RYAN'S CAPITAL ACCOUNT.   Cr.

	£	s.	d.		£	s.	d.
To Cash (withdrawn)	80	0	0	By Sundries (Initial Net			
To Balance,				Capital)... ...	400	0	0
Ryan's Final Net }	853	6	8	„ Profit and Loss, ⅓			
Capital ...				Net Profit ...	533	6	8
	£933	6	8		£933	6	8
				Ryan's Final Net			
				Capital ... ·	£853	6	8

DOE'S CAPITAL ACCOUNT.

	£	s.	d.		£	s.	d.
To Cash (withdrawn)	120	0	0	By Sundries (Initial }			
To Balance,				Net Capital) }	800	0	0
Doe's Final Net }	1,746	13	4	„ P. & L., ⅔ Net }			
Capital.				Profit ... }	1,066	13	4
	£1,866	13	4		£1,866	13	4
				Doe's Final Net }	£1,746	13	4
				Capital }			

ABBREVIATIONS USED IN BUSINESS.

A/C	Account Current.	J. A.	Joint Account.
A/S	Account Sales.	L. B.	Letter Book.
Adv.	Adventure.	L/C	Letter of Credit.
B/E	Bill of Exchange.	M/D	Months after date.
B/L	Bill of Lading.	M/S	Months after sight.
C/C	Cash Credit.	N/P	Net Proceeds.
C/O	Cash Order.	O/A	On Account of.
Comm.	Commission.	P/C	Price Current.
C. I. F.	{ Charges, Insurance, Freight paid.	P/N	Promissory Note.
		P.O.O.	Post Office Order.
Const.	Consignment.	Prox.	{ Proximo, next month.
Dbk.	Drawback.		
D/D	Days after date.	Rect.	Receipt.
D/S	Days after sight.	S/A	Sales Account.
E. E.	Errors excepted.	S/B	Sales Book.
E. & O. E.	{ Errors & omissions excepted.	Stg.	{ Sterling, Good English Money.
F.O.B.	{ Free on board. Carriage paid to ship.	Sqn.	{ Sequestration, Bankruptcy.
Indent	{ Contract ; order for goods.	Ult.	Ultimo, last month.
		Wart'.	Warrants.
Inv.	Invoice or Inventory.	°/₀ per cent. ; °/₀₀ per thousand.	
Inst.	{ Instant ; present month.		

COMMERCIAL BOOKKEEPING: HOW IT DIFFERS FROM THEORETICAL BOOK-KEEPING.

SOME businesses require their own special books. Some require a Stock Book showing separately *quantities* bought and sold. Many need nothing but (1) Waste Book, (2) Purchases Book, (3) Sales Book, (4) Cash Book, and (5) Ledger. Wholesale Houses generally keep a Journal. The main principles of Double-Entry remain the same whatever books are used. The one indispensable book is the Ledger, which contains the essence of all the others collected and classified for ready reference.

In the article on "Compendious or Classified Journalising," the counting-house method of *posting by summary* is shown. As soon as the essential principles have been learnt, the pupil should practise this method with the month's transactions given in various Examination Papers. Instead of posting item by item, as in the Waste Book, he should group together, as one entry, all similar transactions that have taken place during the whole month, referring to the page of the Subsidiary Book from which the summary has been compiled.

The summaries should be entered weekly, instead of monthly, sometimes. This method of grouping together all like transactions falling within a given period (*i.e.* entering as one amount the *total* of all amounts falling on the same side of the same account) saves much time and space, and keeps the Ledger free from all detail not of prime importance.

There are also Trade usages rarely referred to in Theoretical Bookkeeping. For instance, when a Banker, B, discounts a Bill for £400 held by a Merchant, M, and allows him £390 for it, he credits M in his Pass Book with the whole £400, and *debits* him with £10 discount, as interest charged on the £400 credited. M, following the same course, debits his Bank account with the whole £400, and credits his Bills Receivable account with £400 to cancel the £400 asset on its Debit side; he also debits Profit and Loss account £10 to show he has lost £10, and credits his Bank account £10 to indicate that the Banker owes him £10 less than previously recorded, the £10 charged as interest. In Theoretical Bookkeeping, we debit M's Bank account with £390 only, debit Profit and Loss £10, and credit Bills Receivable £400. The two methods differ in form only. The same may be said of every other difference in detail between Theoretical and Commercial Bookkeeping.

GLOSSARY

Of Commercial Terms and Phrases not fully explained in the Text.

Ad Valōrem Duty.—A tax levied according to *value*, not varying with weight, measure, or quantity only, but being more for a pound or a gallon of superior quality than for a pound or a gallon of inferior quality. Thus, the stamp required on a Bill for £500 is 5*s.*, but on one for £3,500 it costs £2; and an Ad Valorem Duty on tea would be twice as much on a pound at 2*s.* as on a pound at 1*s.*

Advance.—(1) Money paid into the business by a partner as loan or additional Capital; (2) Money sent beforehand *by* me in part payment of a Consignment Inwards on its way to me; (3) ditto sent *to* me by Consignee in part payment of a Consignment from me (a Consignment Outwards) shortly expected by him.

Advice.—A business letter announcing some transaction: *e.g.*, from my Banker, announcing that some Acceptances held by me, and sent to him for collection, have been honoured.

Arbitration of Exchange is computing the gain or loss effected by paying a Bill due in St. Petersburg (say) by first changing English money into Dutch at Amsterdam, that into German at Hamburg, and the German into Russian at St. Petersburg.

Audit.—Official examination and testing of accounts.

Bill of Lading.—A captain's signed receipt for merchandise put on board his vessel. It is on stamped paper, and is *negotiable—i.e.*, money can be raised on it as on a Bill. Bills of Lading are drawn, like Foreign Bills, in triplicate; one copy for the captain, one for the consignor or shipper, the third for the consignee.

Bond.—A legal document binding the person who signs it to pay back a debt, or pay a stated Interest on it.

Bonded Goods: Goods in Bond.—Merchandise detained in Government warehouses until the duty on it has been paid.

Bottomry.—A ship mortgage deed. A captain is allowed, in urgent cases, to pledge his vessel to pay for repairing her.

Bullion.—Gold or silver uncoined. Coined money is Specie.

Cash Credit, or Credit Note.—Credit or Loan given by a banker by a draft on another bank.

Charter Party.—A written covenant between the owner of a vessel and the freighter or hirer.

Clearing House.—Where various bankers' representatives meet to pay each other's cheques and to receive payment for them. If A and B are bankers, and A's customers have paid into his bank cheques on B's bank amounting to £5000, while B's customers have paid to B cheques on A's bank amounting to £6000, the whole business is done by A paying B £1000 ; or, what will amount to the same thing when they settle, A credits B's account with £1000.

Consignment Inwards.—Goods sent to me to sell for another at his risk, which I do not bring into Trade account, but record in Consignor's Personal account. In trade a consignment is any goods sent off.

Consignment Outwards.—Goods I send away for another to sell on my account, and at my risk, and for which I open a separate Goods account apart from Trade account.

Coupons.—Certificates of interest at the foot of bonds and debentures, each bearing a different date, showing when the holder is to present it for payment.

Debentures.—(1) Certificates entitling the holder to interest on money lent to companies, corporations, etc. They are transferable like Government Stock. (2) At the Custom House, credit notes given to a merchant who exports goods which he has paid import duty upon. They entitle him to have refunded to him the drawback allowed on re-exported merchandise.

Demurrage.—Allowance made to a shipowner by a freighter for detaining the vessel beyond the time named in the Charty Party.

Dividend.—(1) Interest shared. (2) What a bankrupt pays in the £.

Dock Warrant.—A certificate signed by the dock authorities declaring that the merchandise named on it has been deposited with them.

Draft.—A Cheque, Bill, Promissory Note, or Credit Note.

Drawback.—Money paid back at Custom House. *See* DEBENTURE.

Embargo.—Arrest or confiscation by Government of ships in port.

Exchange.—Changing one country's money for another's : *e.g.*, 100 English sovereigns for 2520 French francs. The *Rate of Exchange* is the *unit* of one country's coinage expressed in terms of the *unit* of another country's : *e.g.*, the par of exchange between Paris and London is expressed by the equation $£1 = 25\frac{1}{5}$ francs. The *Course of Exchange* is the *actual* value of that unit at any particular time as opposed to its *nominal* or par value. Thus, £1 may be worth $25\frac{1}{2}$ fr., then English money is above par, or at a premium. Its value depends (1) on the intrinsic worth of the metal ; and (2) on the demand there is for that particular money at the time. When Bills drawn on London merchants are plentiful in Paris, their holders in Paris wishing to get francs for them will sell them more cheaply on that account—*i.e.*, more English money for the same number of francs ; a Bill on London for more than £100 for 2520 francs. The Course of Exchange is then in favour of France, and against England—against the country that would have to remit more gold than the other if there were no paper money.

Exchequer Bills.—Bills drawn on Government payable with interest at the Bank of England, to bankers and others who have lent money to the country. They are Bills of Credit issued by the Treasury under authority of Parliament, and form the unfunded part of the National Debt. The funded part is never repaid directly, except as Terminable Annuities, which mean increased interest during the stockholder's life, and then extinction of the debt or stock. Much of the National Debt is being thus paid off.

Folio.—The Dr. and the Cr. sides of an account; sometimes two pages, sometimes one : generally two in Cash Book.

Funds, Stock, Consols.—Debts which Government owes to the various stockholders : the chief part of the National Debt. No certificate is issued, but every holder of stock is registered in the Bank of England books as a Government creditor. The loan is never repaid, but interest on it accrues at a fixed rate, and it can be sold at a price varying with the demand for it.

Gazetted.—Officially registered as a bankrupt in the *London Gazette*.

Hypothecation.—Mortgaging or pledging a vessel. *See* BOTTOMRY.

Insurance Policy.—The written agreement between a shipowner and the underwriters or insurance company. The premium is the money paid by the owner.

Legal Tender.—Offered payment valid in law. Bronze up to 1*s.*; silver up to 40*s.*; gold and Bank of England notes to any amount are good offers.

Letter of Credit.—Draft on a Bank; or a letter addressed by a London merchant (say) to his agent in Australia (say) requesting him to pay bearer a specified sum on presenting the letter.

Limited.—If A holds one of one hundred shares in a Limited Liability Company, he cannot be called upon to pay more than $\frac{1}{100}$ part of the deficit in the Balance Sheet if the Company fail. His liability is limited to the same fraction of the whole Liability that his part of the Capital was of the whole Capital. Sometimes his liability is limited to what remains unpaid on his shares. Besides these limitations by *shares*, there may be limitation by *guarantee*, as specified on the Memorandum of Association.

Negotiable; A Negotiable Instrument.—Transferable or saleable by endorsement. Bills, Bills of Lading, etc., can be endorsed for value received, and then belong to the endorsee.

Par.—Latin for "equal." Stock is at par when £100 cash will buy £100 of stock. Exchange is at par between England and France when £1 counts as 25·20 francs; when the *actual* value of the monetary unit agrees with the *nominal* value.

Per pro ▬ per procuration, in place of; acting as representative of. When a clerk or manager named Thomas Grover signs a settled account, he writes thus :—

    Per pro Rylands & Co., Thomas Grover.

Power of Attorney.—A legal document empowering one person to act for another in signing cheques, accepting and endorsing Bills, etc. The authorising party then becomes responsible for what he does.

Price Current.—List of goods for sale with prices up to date.

Real Estate.—Lands and houses; immovable property. Money, paper money (shares, Consols, etc.), furniture, and movable property of every kind, form the *Personal Estate.* "*Probate*" is a certified copy of deceased's will, and the certificate from Somerset House declaring the will proved and the probate duty paid.

Re Smith.—In the matter or business of Smith.

Salvage.—Allowance made to those who save goods from wreckage or fire.

Sequestration.—Bankruptcy.

Short Bills.—Bills payable at sight, or within a few days.

Specie.—Coin; not paper money, nor gold in bars.

Voucher.—Evidence proving the truth of an item: *e.g.,* receipts showing cash paid, title deeds proving assets named, acceptances in hand showing debts acknowledged.

APPENDIX.

NOTE I.

A Final Asset or a Final Liability from the Profit and Loss Accounts.

IT occasionally happens that I cannot represent my financial position quite truthfully, on closing books, without crediting one or more of the Profit and Loss accounts and debiting the same sum to Valuation account as a *final Asset*; or I may have to debit one of the Profit and Loss accounts and credit the same amount to Valuation or some other account as a *final Liability*. This may arise from my having over-debited one of the Profit and Loss accounts, or from not having debited it enough. If I have debited Trade Expenses £40 for horse fodder, of which only £10 worth has been consumed, I have an asset of £30 in the remaining food, and so credit Trade Expenses £30 to cancel the over-debit, and credit Valuation account £30 as a final Asset for Final Balance Sheet. So with any *Reserve Fund*. If I set aside £100 as a provision for future bad debts by debiting Profit and Loss £100 and crediting Reserve Fund £100, but find when I close books that my actual loss from bad debts has been but £20, I am £80 better off than my books represent. I therefore credit Profit and Loss £80 to correct the over-debit, and debit Reserve Fund £80, thus closing that account by virtually adding an asset of £80. If I pay £20 for a typewriter, and instead of

126

debiting it to Valuation account as a permanent asset I debit it as a dead loss to Profit and Loss, I put among the expenses of one year what ought to be divided amongst eight or ten years. I correct the error by crediting Profit and Loss at the year's end with £18, say, allowing £2 for depreciation, and debit Valuation account £18 as a final asset. On the other hand, if I close my books on November 30th, and ignore the heavy Trade Expenses in rent, wages, gas, etc., which I shall have to pay in December, I do not accurately represent my affairs; so I debit a part of these to Profit and Loss and credit Outstanding Liabilities account with the same amount.

These entries may be regarded as corrections of over-debits, or as immediate records instead of deferred ones, rather than as exceptions to what has been said in the article on *the unique double character of Trade account.*

NOTE II.

Caution as to the Terms "Acceptance" and "Draft."

Though the same piece of stamped paper, with the Acceptor's name across it and the Drawer's name at its foot, is both an Acceptance and a Draft, yet "my Acceptance for £100" and "my Draft for £100" are very different things indeed, and mistaking one for the other would make a difference of *twice* £100 in my Final Balance Sheet. A Bill is the Acceptance of the Debtor, who *accepts* it by writing his name across it; it is the Draft of the Creditor, who *draws* on the Acceptor. My Acceptance is a Liability of mine, a Bill Payable in my books. My Draft is an Asset of mine, a Bill Receivable in my books. If

I owe Smith £500, and he draws on me for that sum, the Bill he writes is Smith's draft on me; when I accept it, by signing it, it becomes my Acceptance for £500, a Liability of mine, an Asset of Smith's. If Jones owes me £200, and I draw on him for that sum, the Bill I make out is my draft on Jones for £200; when Jones has accepted it, by signing it, it becomes Jones's Acceptance, a Liability of his, an Asset of mine. Learners must carefully note these expressions, and remember that, until honoured, my own Acceptances are in the possession of my creditors as evidence of what I owe them. The drawers keep their Drafts on me, as I keep mine when I have drawn on my debtors.